AMERICA'S EAR
ADVERTISING PAPER DULLƆ

Lagretta Metzger Bajorek

Photographs Benjamin T. Bajorek

"Crown" Piano!
Oh! Yes, that's the one which has
many tones.
"Mama says no other is like or
equal to it."

Schiffer Publishing Ltd

4880 Lower Valley Road, Atglen, PA 19310 USA

Dedication

To my husband, Ben, for his work and patience in photographing the many, many dolls.

U. S. CAVALRY PRIVATE.

Designed by Randy L. Hensley
Type set in University Roman Bd/Times New Roman

ISBN: 0-7643-0702-9
Printed in China
1234

Published by Schiffer Publishing Ltd.
4880 Lower Valley Road
Atglen, PA 19310
Phone: (610) 593-1777; Fax: (610) 593-2002
E-mail: Schifferbk@aol.com
Please visit our web site catalog at www.schifferbooks.com
or write for a free catalog.
This book may be purchased from the publisher.
Please include $3.95 for shipping.

In Europe, Schiffer books are distributed by
Bushwood Books
6 Marksbury Rd.
Kew Gardens
Surrey TW9 4JF England
Phone: 44 (0)181 392-8585; Fax: 44 (0)181 392-9876
E-mail: Bushwd@aol.com

Please try your bookstore first.

We are interested in hearing from authors
with book ideas on related subjects.

Contents

Acknowledgements

My special thanks to my brother-in-law, Paul Rieger, for his help and all the useful advice he gave to me.

I am grateful to Virginia Crossley and my sister, Loretta Rieger, for sharing their paper dolls.

I am also thankful to my sister, Loretta, who traveled with me through the many years in search of paper dolls. We shared some good times "hunting" together.

My appreciation for the help I received from my Creative Writing Class and our instructor Arlene Teed.

Many thanks to my editor, Molly Higgins, and the Schiffer Publishing organization for an opportunity to see my paper doll collection in print.

Value Guide

The majority of die-cut advertising dolls are 5-1/2" in height. An ordinary individual doll of this size from a series of dolls is usually priced from $6–$12 due to condition and coloring.

A cut set of a cutout doll has a lesser value than an uncut set.

At one time the rule of thumb was to double the price of a series if it was complete, but at today's prices the collectible world is more driven by demand and the rarity of a piece.

The following prices are based on the author's personal experience, paper doll shows, paper doll dealers' lists, auctions, and collectible conventions, except where she was unable to set a realistic price for rare sets.

Disclaimer

The current values listed in this book should be used only as a guide. Prices vary from one section of the country to another and are affected by condition, color of prints, and the completeness of sets or series. Neither the author nor the publisher assumes responsibility for any losses which might be incurred as a result of using this guide.

Preservation

One very important feature about collecting anything made of paper is the proper storage and preservation of those paper items. The best guidelines to follow in this regard are those set forth in a leaflet issued by the Library of Congress, entitled "Environmental Protection of Books and Related Material."

That leaflet states "...paper is always subject to deterioration if it is improperly made or stored. At the same time, under proper conditions paper may last for hundreds of years."

Further, "extensive research and a wealth of accumulated evidence show that the lower the temperature at which it is stored, the longer paper will last. ... for every 10°F decrease in temperature, the useful life of paper is approximately doubled. ... For most homes and libraries practical considerations dictate a temperature range of 68° to 75°F."

"Humidity also has a serious effect on ... paper. If too high, it hastens acid deterioration and leads to deterioration by such biological agents as mold and bacteria. If too low, the paper suffers from desiccation" (drying up). Paper "will last longer if kept at a relative humidity of 40 to 50 percent."

Moreover, "there is some evidence that regular changes in temperature and relative humidity (cycling) can lead to a weakening of paper ... Library of Congress scientists do not believe that it results in measurable damage to paper if such changes in temperature and relative humidity can be held to less than 10°F and 15 percent."

Thus, all collectors of paper items, especially items made from pulp paper and cardboard, need to keep their material in a room where both temperature and relative humidity can be regulated within the limitations described by the Library of Congress. This should never be in an attic or basement, but rather a location where the heat duct can be turned off in the winter, and where the effect of air conditioning can be brought to bear during the summer. Also, the use of a humidifier in the winter and a dehumidifier in the summer in the storage area will be of much help

Equally important in the preservation of paper is the enclosure in which the paper itself is stored. The worst enclosure is anything made of vinyl, because the chemicals in that form of plastic can decompose and emit a vapor after several years that will cause the paper to deteriorate. The best enclosures are those made of either Mylar or polypropylene. If albums are used, only those with acid-free paper should be employed. Safe enclosures and albums can be obtained from library and archival supply houses.

These precautionary measures, which are not difficult to follow, apply to collections of any size. They are much less costly in the long run, and will assure many hours of enjoyment for both contemporary and future collectors.

Introduction

Behind an attic door in some old homes one may find a Victorian scrap album filled with old advertising trade and insert cards, a medium once used by innumerable manufacturers and merchants to advertise and promote their products.

"The Golden Age" of the advertising trade card was in the 1880s–1890s. With the advent of color lithography—the transfer printing process in which the color image is transferred to the paper from inked flat stones or metal plates—printers began to produce large quantities of inexpensive colorful lithographic prints. In the 1890s, advertising became a large industry, as color lithography became more widespread and the mail service provided an efficient means of distribution.

Tobacco

At this time, the idea of packaging advertising trade cards with a manufacturer's product was first developed by tobacco companies, and later it spread to other commodities. These trade cards, some in the form of paper dolls and paper toys, were issued as premiums that were packaged with the products or were sent through the mail in exchange either for the company's coupons or for one coupon and a few pennies worth of U.S. postage stamps.

The Banner Tobacco Co., Detroit (Night Watch/Pippin Cut Plug Tobacco)

"Two of the best and most reliable brands made, always uniform and reliable."

The Banner Tobacco Company issued a "Mother Goose" series of 12 cutout dolls in color lithography with front and back costumes. The dolls were sent in exchange for 12 coupons or, if one could not collect all 12 coupons, one coupon and six cents in U.S. postage stamps.

The series consisted of Sinbad the Sailor, Little Bo-Peep, Jack, Jill, Cinderella, Little Boy Blue, Aladdin, Mother Hubbard, Jack the Giant Killer, Sleeping Beauty, Red Riding Hood and Puss in Boots.

This "Mother Goose" series is known as a stock set, a set that a lithographer sold to many companies with a different company's advertisement printed on each set of dolls. The advantage of a stock set is that it allows a collector to complete a series using advertisements from several companies.

Several examples of companies which used the "Mother Goose" series for advertisements were Hershey's Chocolate, Robinson's Flavoring Extracts, Enterprise Coffee, Cordova Coffee, The Standard Sewing Machine Co., Miller's Organ, Capital Coffee, and Ohio Coffee & Spice Co.

Banner Tobacco Company, "Mother Goose," series, "Red Riding Hood," c.1890. $18-20

Banner Tobacco Co., "Mother Goose," series. Left to right: Row 1. (top), Sinbad the Sailor, Little Bo-Peep, Jack, Jill, Cinderella, Little Boy Blue. Row 2. Aladdin, Mother Hubbard, Jack the Giant Killer, Sleeping Beauty, Red Riding Hood, and Puss in Boots. Stock set $125

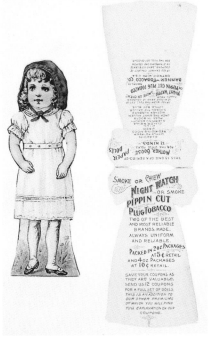

Banner Tobacco Co., "Red Riding Hood," reversed.

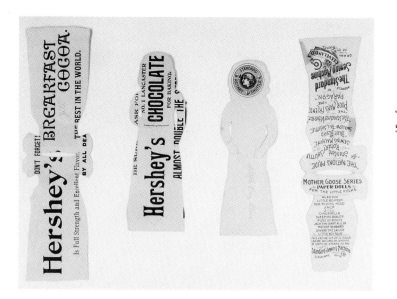

"Mother Goose," series, Hershey's Chocolate and Standard Sewing Machine advertisements.

Blackwell's Durham Tobacco Co., Durham, North Carolina

"Blackwell's Genuine Durham Smoking Tobacco"

Another company which issued cutout dolls was Blackwell's Durham Tobacco Company. Its dolls were "The Fashion Dolls," copyrighted 1895, printed in color lithography. This was a set of 91 pieces, and consisted of six dolls: mother, two daughters, one little girl, one boy, and one French nurse with a baby, along with their wardrobes. The set was mailed for six coupons secured from bags of Blackwell's Durham Tobacco. Other paper toys offered as premiums by this company were farm buildings, animals, and Durham's Circus.

Paper dolls and paper toys issued by tobacco companies are rare, because premiums from these companies were mainly pictures of "fine ladies of the theater," to entice smokers to buy their brand and collect the entire series of pictures.

Blackwell's Durham Tobacco Company, "The Fashion Dolls,"1895, sample issue. $75

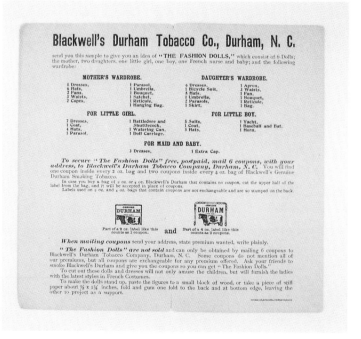

Blackwell's Durham Tobacco Co., "The Fashion Dolls," sample issue reversed.

8

Patent Medicine

Between 1865 and the 1890s most American families had their own home medical books and their own supply of folk medicines and root remedies. With the growth of the advertising industry, many newspapers and magazines near the beginning of the 20th century started to publish medical advertisements praising the various "cures" of patent medicine, which also appeared on the contemporary paper dolls. These pronouncements, however, were without the proper follow-through of scientific reliability for medical claims, and thus a concerned Congress in 1906 passed the Pure Food and Drug Act, prohibiting the word "cure" from being used on advertisements for patent medicine.

Because of the controversy over the use of the word "cure," patent medicine companies began to use words such as "remedy", "harmless" and "relief." Then, as advertising claims and testimonials became more outrageous, a few of the businesses involved started enforcing standards of truth, and later the Pure Food and Drug Act of 1938 broadened the power of the Federal Trade Commission to enforce truth in advertising.

The C. I. Hood & Co., Lowell, Massachusetts.

*"I am So Nervous
Hood's Sarsaparilla Cures"*

Hood offered a family of five paper dolls to promote their patent medicine. This set of dolls comes in several variations.

The print on the back of the sample hat reads: "Full set of 17 pieces in beautiful colors, sent for one trade-mark from Hood's Pills and 10 cents in stamps."

These dolls and their costumes are known as die-cuts because they were cut from the paper at the print shop using a mechanical die. They were issued in 1894, in color lithography. The dolls consisted of the father, mother, two daughters, and a son. The dolls' hats were the only items that had to be cut.

The word "cure" appears many times in the advertising claims on the reverse side of the set. The boxes which the father and son hold are for Hood's Sarsaparilla patent medicine.

The print on the front of the sample doll reads: "Full set of 19 pieces for one trade-mark from Hood's Pills and 10 cents in stamps." This 19-piece set has an extra die-cut plaid costume and another hat for one of the daughters. As in the 17-piece set, the hats are the only items that had to be cut.

The Hood's Sarsaparilla Calendar for 1897 had a redeemable May 1st coupon, which together with ten cents in postage stamps could be used to obtain Hood's Paper Doll Family of 19 pieces.

The company used the same five die-cut dolls, but costumes and hats varied in design and colors for a more up-to-date wardrobe, except for the father's tan coat which had a box of Hood's Sarsaparilla showing out of his pocket. There were special cutting instructions printed on the front of each die-cut doll. For example, printed on the father's chest were the following directions: "Cut through the card on heavy black outlines of whiskers."

There is evidence of yet another variation of the set having been issued. Four known little girls' hats different in design from any other set has been acknowledged to belong to Hood's paper dolls.

Hood readily complied with the sentiments of the Pure Food and Drug Act. A 1905 wrap-a-round red dressed die-cut baby doll, in color lithography, holding a box of Hood's Sarsaparilla medicine did not have the word "cure" but instead claimed to be "the greatest remedy in the world".

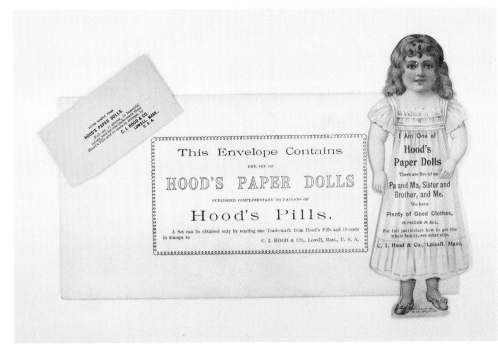

C. I. Hood & Company, envelope, sample hat, and sample doll. $5 (hat), $20 (doll)

Hood's Family,
1894. $185
(envelope)

Hood's Family,
costumes for mother
and father.

Hood's Family,
costumes for
daughters.

Hood's Family, costumes for son.

Hood's Calendar, 1897, paper doll coupon. $25

C. I. Hood & Co., advertisements for the word "cure," mother and daughter reversed.

Hood's baby doll, reversed.

C.I. Hood & Co., baby doll, 1905. $25-30

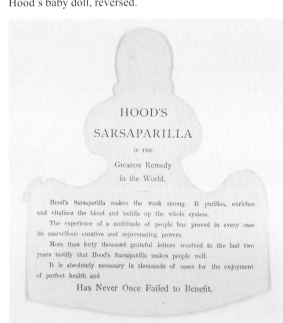

Dr. J. C. Ayer & Co., Lowell Massachusetts

*"Cures others, will cure you.
Ayer's Cherry Pectoral, Medal and Diploma
at World's Fair."*

The company advertised that Ayer's was the only sarsaparilla admitted at the World's Fair, Chicago, in 1893. In 1894, Ayer's Sarsaparilla issued, in color lithography produced by the Gast Lithography & Engraving Co., New York, a die-cut "Doll Bride," with the word "cure" in its advertisements.

The doll had clever reversible arms with long gloves, and the costumes were reversible: bridal gown/party dress, spring dress/winter dress, hats, and wedding veil. The doll was mailed to any address on receipt of twelve cents in postage stamps.

Later, Ayer's gave out a stand-up set of die-cut paper dolls in color lithography, for the "House That Jack Built."

The set consisted of 11 pieces: Jack's house with the nursery rhyme on the reverse side; the malt which laid in the house; the elusive rat (which is usually missing in a set, as the piece is very small); the cat that killed the rat; the dog that worried the cat; the cow with the crumpled horn; the maiden all forlorn; Jack all tattered and torn; the priest all shaven and shorn; the cock that crowed in the morn; and the man who owned the farm, who sowed the grain.

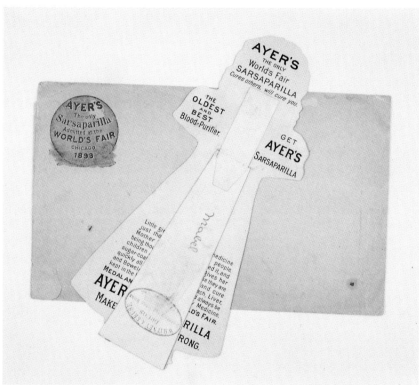

J. C. Ayer & Company, the only sarsaparilla at the World's Fair, 1893, advertisement.

Ayer's "Doll Bride," 1894, and wedding dress (all costumes are reversible). $125 (envelope)

Ayer's Doll Bride, spring and party dresses.

Ayer's Doll Bride, winter dress.

J.C. Ayer & Company, "The House That Jack Built." $125-150 (envelope)

Dr. R. V. Pierce, Buffalo, New York

"Cure sick headache,..." Dr. Pierce's Pleasant Pellets, a vegetable compound for distrubances of the system.

"... made a record in the cure of bronchial, throat and lung diseases." Golden Medical Discovery, a highly nutritive and tonic compound preparation.

Dr. Pierce wrote many books on health, one of which, *The People's Common Sense Medical Adviser*, sold over a million copies. He also managed the Invalid's Hotel and Surgical Institute, as well as The World's Dispensary Medical Association, both in Buffalo.

Dr. Pierce's die-cut head-and-shoulder dolls in color lithography used the word "cure" in their advertisements. The dolls are from a common stock set which were used by many companies, such as the Cortland Beef Company, Cortland, New York.

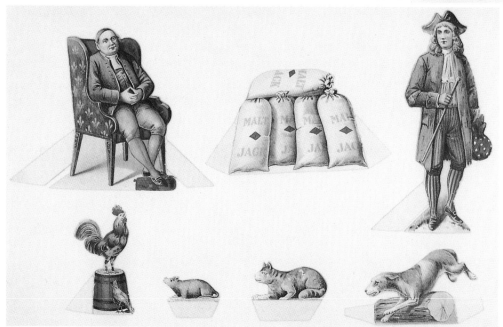

TOP: Dr. R. V. Pierce, c.1890. $15 each

CENTER LEFT: Ayer's "The House That Jack Built," the man, cow and maiden.

CENTER RIGHT: Dr. Pierce's advertisements for Pleasant Pellets and Golden Medical Discovery with the word "cure."

BOTTOM: Ayer's "The House That Jack Built," the priest, malt, Jack, cock, rat, cat and dog.

Orangeine, The Orangeine Chemical Co., Chicago

"First Step to Health
Prevents and Cures Hay Fever and Asthma..."

The company had two die-cut dolls, a mother and daughter in color lithography. The Orangeine advertisement in the June 1906 Sears, Roebuck and Co. Drug Catalog, however, did not use the word "cure". The catalog price read, "Regular 25 cent size; our price 19 cents."

Jayne's Tonic Vermifuge, Dr. D. Jayne, Philadelphia

"Cures dyspepsia, indigestion, and tones the stomach."

In 1895 this company issued easel cutout dolls in color lithography, using "cure" in their advertisements. They are referred to as easel dolls because when all of the garment pieces are fitted correctly by the numbers printed on each piece, the doll will stand erect, just as an easel is supported. The advertisements remain on the back of each piece when the doll is cut.

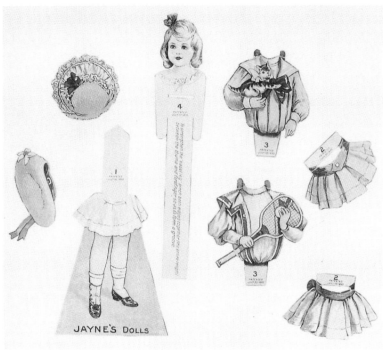

Orangeine Chemical Co., Orangeine's mother and daughter. $30

Jayne's Tonic Vermifuge, blond doll, 1895. $15

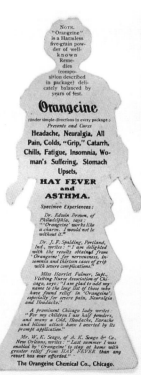

Jayne's Tonic Vermifuge, brunette doll, 1895, reversed advertisement uses the word "cure." $12 as shown

Orangeine's mother, reversed, advertisement uses "prevents" and "cure."

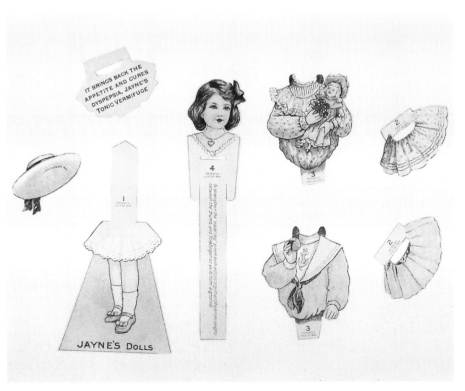

Pozzoni's Complexion Powder, J. A. Pozzoni Pharmacal Co., St. Louis, MO

"Mamma thinks there is nothing like Pozzoni's Powder."

Starting about 1880, "new" immigrants to the United States, those from southern and eastern Europe, began to outnumber "old" immigrants, people who had come from England, Ireland, Germany, and the Scandanavian countries. By 1896, America had truly become a nation of many nationalities, and thus companies at this time and through the turn of the century, began to use ethnic paper doll sets as premiums in their advertising.

J.A. Pozzoni Pharmacal Company offered an ethnic set of 16 die-cut head-and-shoulder dolls named "Native Costumes and National Emblems." The complete set was mailed upon receipt of six cents in postage.

The countries represented in the set were America, England, Ireland, Scotland, Holland, France, Germany, Switzerland, Austria, Italy, Spain, Mexico, Turkey, Russia, China, and Japan.

Because these dolls in color lithography were a stock set, they were issued as advertisements for other companies, some of which were outside the industry of patent medicines. Examples are Merrick's Spool Cotton; Doll Soap, Allen B. Wrisley Co., Chicago; and Sarica Coffee, from The Tracy & Avery Co., Mansfield, Ohio.

Pozzoni's Complexion Powder, "Native Costumes and National Emblems," Austria. $10-12

Pozzoni's "Native Costumes and National Emblems." Left to right: Row l. (top), America, England, Holland, France, Germany, Switzerland. Row 2. Austria, Italy, Spain, Mexico, Turkey, China and Japan. (Ireland, Scotland and Russia are not pictured) Stock set $130 as shown

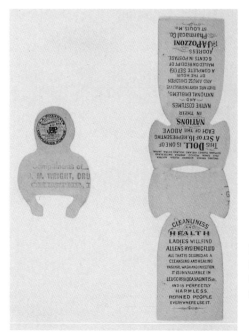

Pozzoni's trademark, and inside advertisement on a doll's dress.

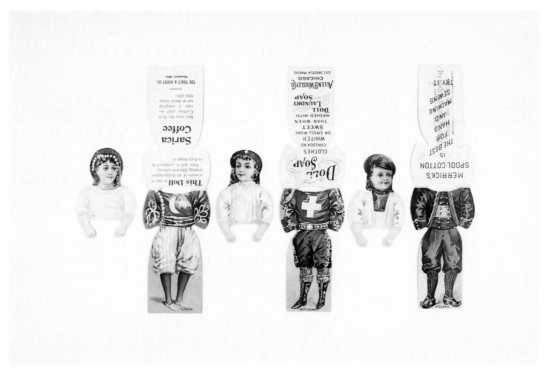

"Native Costumes and National Emblems," Sarica Coffee, Doll Soap
and Merrick's Spool Cotton, advertisements. $8-10 each

Beecham's Pills, B. F. Allen Co., New York

"Constipation causes more than half the sickness in the world, especially in women.
10¢ and 25¢ a box"

The company issued a set of six die-cut head-and-shoulder paper dolls in color lithography in different designs. A set of these dolls was mailed upon receipt of five cents.

Other companies offered dolls advertising their medical claims included The Kickapoo Indian Medicine Co., New Haven, Connecticut; Dr. Mile's Medical Company, Elkart, Indiana; and Minard's Liniment Company, Framingham, Massachusetts.

Beecham's Pills, B.F. Allen Co. $12 each

Beverages

"Little Red Ridinghood was my first love. I felt that if I could have married Little Red Ridinghood I should have known perfect bliss."
Charles Dickens (1812-1870)

Influenced by the rising tide of nationalism in Germany early in the 1800s, the Grimm brothers began to collect the legends and folk lore of their countrymen. "Little Red Ridinghood" was one of the treasured tales that the Grimm brothers perserved in its rich, original charm and fantasy.

There are many characters from fairy tales and folk tales represented in issues of the advertising paper dolls.

Lion Coffee, "Nursery Rhyme Dolls, "Little Red Riding Hood," #4. $45

Coffee

Fortunately, coffee joined the group of advertising trade and insert card issuers. Because not all packaged coffee had national distribution, paper doll sets from coffee companies were often limited in their circulation. The two leaders in the issuance of insert cards in the 1890s were Woolson Spice Co., Toledo, Ohio, makers of Lion Coffee, and McLaughlin Coffee, Chicago, Illinois. Their paper doll sets have become very popular with collectors.

Lion Coffee, Woolson Spice Co., Toledo, Ohio

"The Workingman's Friend"

A paper doll die-cut set depicting "Little Red Riding Hood" was offered as a premium by Lion Coffee. The four-piece set printed in color lithography was from their series of "Nursery Rhyme Dolls." They also had two other series, "Occupations," and "A Doll House," and each had 16 die-cut four-piece sets in color lithography.

Lion Coffee, "A Doll House," advertisement reversed.

Lion Coffee, "A Doll House," advertisement. $20

Lion Coffee, Woolson Spice Company, "Nursery Rhyme Dolls," advertisement. $20

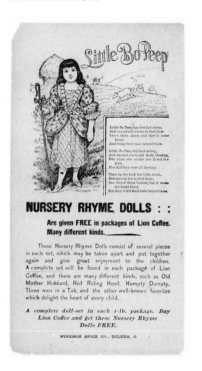

Lion Coffee, "Little Red Riding Hood," reversed.

The name Lion Coffee and a set number appears on the front of each piece, while on the reverse side there is an advertisement, and a title for all three series. Set numbers are also printed on the reverse side of the "Nursery Rhyme Dolls" and "Occupations" series. The reverse of the background piece in all sets shows a line drawing of the complete set for easy identification. The "Nursery Rhyme Dolls" have an appropriate nursery rhyme on the background piece. The "Doll House" series advertisement states that a set was given free in each package of Lion Coffee.

Lion Coffee, "Old King Cole," #1. $45

Lion Coffee, "Old Mother Hubbard," #2. $45

19

Lion Coffee, "Mother Goose," #3. $45

Lion Coffee, "Little Boy Blue," #5. $45

Lion Coffee, "Little Bo-Peep," #6. $45

Lion Coffee, "Jack and Jill," #7. $45

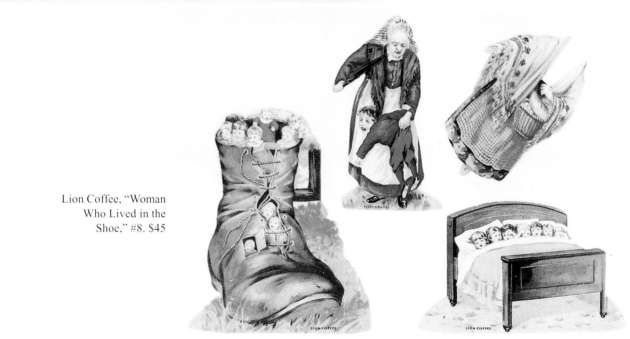

Lion Coffee, "Woman Who Lived in the Shoe," #8. $45

Lion Coffee, "Rub-A-Dub-Dub," #10. $45

Lion Coffee. "Humpty Dumpty," #9. $45

Lion Coffee, "Little Jack Horner," #11. $45

Lion Coffee, "Mary Had A Little Lamb," #12. $45

Lion Coffee, "Simple Simon," #13. $45

Lion Coffee, "Ding-Dong-Bell," #14. $45

Lion Coffee, "The Queen of Hearts," #16. $45

Lion Coffee, "Sing a Song of Sixpence," #15. $45

Lion Coffee, Woolson Spice Co., "Occupations," series, "The Miller," #1. $45

Lion Coffee, "The Miller," reversed.

Lion Coffee, "The Barber," #2. $40 as shown

Lion Coffee, "The Gardner," #3. $45

Lion Coffee, "The
Carpenter," #4. $45

Lion Coffee, "The Tailor,"
#5. $40 as shown

Lion Coffee, "The Mason," #6.
$40 as shown

Lion Coffee, "The Shoemaker," #7. $45

Lion Coffee, "The Photographer," #8. $45

Lion Coffee, "The Butcher," #9. $45

Lion Coffee, "The Blacksmith," #10. $45

Lion Coffee, "The Cooper," #11. $45

Lion Coffee, "The Baker," #12. $45

Lion Coffee, "The Printer," #13. $45

Lion Coffee, "The Bicycle Maker," #14. $45

Lion Coffee, "The Milliner," #15. $45

Lion Coffee, "The
Grocer," #16. $45

Lion Coffee, Woolson Spice
Co., "A Doll House," series,
"The Bedroom," #1. $45

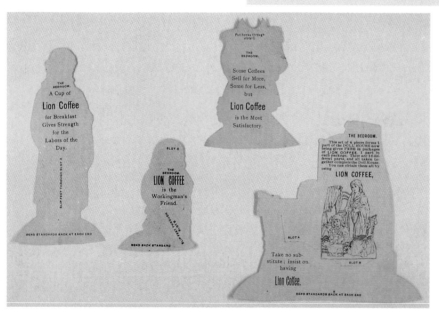

Lion Coffee, "The
Bedroom," reversed.

Lion Coffee, "The Lawn," #2. $45

Lion Coffee, "The Nursery," #3. $45

Lion Coffee, "The Bath Room," #4. $45

Lion Coffee, "The Library," #5. $45

Lion Coffee, "The Park," #6. $45

Lion Coffee, "The Dining Room," #7. $45

Lion Coffee, "The Furnace Room," #8. $45

Lion Coffee, "The Garden," #9. $45

Lion Coffee, "The Lake," #10. $45

Lion Coffee, "The Butler's Pantry," #11. $45

Lion Coffee, "The Hall," #12. $45

Lion Coffee, "The Laundry," #13. $45

Lion Coffee, "The Stable," #15. $45

Lion Coffee, "The Music Room," #16. $45

Lion Coffee, "The Kitchen," #14. $45

In 1892 and 1895, Lion Coffee gave a "Brownie" paper doll in each package of their coffee. The advertisement on the back of the "Standing Brownie" was printed in both English and German, because at that time there were many German-speaking citizens, and advertisers sought their trade.

The Brownies, which were stand-up dolls, were unnumbered and were from two different die-cut sets of Palmer Cox's Brownies, known as "The Standing Brownies" and "The Riding Brownies." Palmer Cox (1840-1924) was an author and illustrator, famous for his children's classic "Brownie" books.

The Brownie dolls in the first series had detachable heads, while in the second series the Brownie dolls were the detachable riders. Both series were printed in color lithography by H. A. Thomas and Wylie, Lithographers, New York, by permission of Arnold Print Works, North Adams, Massachusetts.

Lion Coffee, Indian on Panther and Indian. $45 each

Lion Coffee, Englishman on Fox and Englishman. $45 each

Lion Coffee, Woolson Spice Co., Palmer Cox's Brownies, Uncle Sam on Bison and Uncle Sam. $50 each

Lion Coffee, Dude on Donkey and Dude. $45 each

Lion Coffee, Uncle Sam and Uncle Sam on Bison, reversed.

Lion Coffee, King on Lion and King. $45 and $16 as shown

Lion Coffee, Sailor on Sea Lion and Sailor. $45 each

Lion Coffee, Russian on Wolf and Russian. $45 each

Lion Coffee, Esquimau on Polar Bear and Esquimau. $45 and $20 as shown

Lion Coffee, Irishman on Pig and Irishman. $45 each

Lion Coffee, German Peasant on St. Bernard Dog and German Peasant. $45 each

Lion Coffee, Canadian on Moose and Canadian. $45 each

Lion Coffee, Chinaman on Tiger and Chinaman. $45 each

Lion Coffee, Turk on Camel and Turk. $45 each

Lion Coffee, Policeman on Rhinoceros and Policeman. $45 and $20 as shown

Lion Coffee, East Indian on Elephant and East Indian. $25 as shown and $45

Lion Coffee, Soldier on Kangaroo and Soldier. $45 each

Lion Coffee, Japanese on Zebu and Japanese. $45 each

Lion Coffee, Jockey on Horse and Jockey. $45 each

Lion Coffee, French on Chamois and Spainard on Bull. $45 each

Lion Coffee, Sage on Giraffe and Sage. $45 each

Lion Coffee, Dunce and Student. $20 and $16 as shown

Lion Coffee, Italian on Sheep. $45

Lion Coffee issued two different die-cut series in color lithography entitled "Children's Dolls With Stories," which were given in each package of their coffee. These series of stand-up one-piece dolls, were stated to contain 20 and the other 30.

The set of 30, however, may merely be an extension, by ten, of the set of 20 dolls, inasmuch as only 10 dolls have been located for the set of "30 dolls." Each had the advertisement and the appropriate story printed on the reverse side of each doll.

Lion Coffee, Plain Brownie and Scotchman. $16 as shown and $45

Lion Coffee, Woolson Spice and Co., "Children's Dolls With Stories." *Courtesy of Loretta Metzger Rieger.* $6-10 each

Lion Coffee, Dutchman on Black Bear and Dutchman. $45 each

Lion Coffee, "Children's Dolls With Stories," (The Three Bears and Little Red Riding Hood) reversed. *Courtesy of Loretta Metzger Rieger.*

Lion Coffee, "Children's Dolls With Stories," series of twenty, Left to right: Row 1. (top) Little Red Riding Hood, Blue Beard, Cinderella, Hop O' My Thumb & His Seven League Boots, Aladdin. Row 2. Jack the Giant Killer, Rip Van Winkle, Robinson Crusoe, Puss in Boots, and Jack and the Beanstock. *Courtesy of Loretta Metzger Rieger.* $6-10 each

Lion Coffee, "Children's Dolls With Stories," series of twenty, Left to right: Row 1. (top) Old Mother Hubbard, Little Miss Muffet, Little Jack Horner, Little Boy Blue, Little Bo-Peep. Row 2. Tom, Tom the Piper's Son, Old King Cole, Sinbad the Sailor, Tom Thumb, and Mother Goose. *Courtesy of Loretta Metzger Rieger.* $6-10 each

Lion Coffee, "Children's Dolls With Stories," second set of ten, Left to right: Row 1. (top) Little Snow White, The Frog Prince, Ali Baba, Humpty Dumpty, Mary Quite Contrary, John Gilpin's Ride. Row 2. Yankee Doodle, The Three Bears, Old Woman in the Shoe, and Sleeping Beauty. *Courtesy of Loretta Metzger Rieger.* $6-10 each

McLaughlin Coffee, Chicago,

"Best quality coffee on the market"

During this time McLaughlin Coffee offered many die-cut advertising paper dolls in color lithography as premiums inserted in each package of their coffee. They issued great quantities of dolls, which usually varied in construction from those given by other companies. They had three series which were constructed to be able to sit or stand: "Nursery Rhymes," "Queens," and "Victorian Ladies." All were printed by J. Ottmann Lith. Co., New York.

The "Nursery Rhyme" series had eight die-cut four-piece sets. The name of the coffee company was printed on the front of each piece, and the name of the set was printed on the doll. On the reverse side of each doll was a drawing of the furniture, with directions for assemblage, and an advertisement. This series featured Red Ridinghood.

McLaughlin Coffee, "Nursery Rhyme," series, "Red Riding Hood." $40

McLaughlin Coffee, "Red Riding Hood," reversed.

McLaughlin Coffee, "Miss Muffet." $40

41

McLaughlin Coffee,
"Piper's Son." $40

McLaughlin Coffee,
"Cinderella." $30 as shown

McLaughlin Coffee, "Little Boy
Blue." $30 as shown

McLaughlin Coffee, "Mother Hubbard." $30 as shown

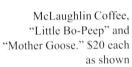

McLaughlin Coffee, "Little Bo-Peep" and "Mother Goose." $20 each as shown

The "Queens," an eight-doll series, consisted of Martha Washington, the first lady of the United States, Marie Antoinette of France, Crown Princess of Sweden, Queen Marguerite of Italy, Czarina of Russia, Queen Elizabeth of England, Queen Isabella of Spain, and Mary Queen of Scots.

Each set has a doll, costume (crown optional) and a piece of furniture. On the reverse side of each doll is a line drawing of the furniture for the set, and directions for assemblage.

McLaughlin Coffee, "Martha Washington and the Queens," Martha Washington, the first lady. $35

McLaughlin Coffee, "Martha Washington," reversed, line drawing of furniture.

McLaughlin Coffee, "Marie Antoinette." $35

McLaughlin Coffee, "Crown Princess of Sweden." $35

McLaughlin Coffee, "Queen Marguerite of Italy." $35

McLaughlin Coffee, "Czarina of Russia." $35

McLaughlin Coffee, "Queen Elizabeth of England." $20 as shown

McLaughlin Coffee, "Queen Isabella of Spain" and "Mary Queen of Scots." $12-15 each

The "Victorian Ladies" series were upper-class women wearing a choker collar or a necklace. Each doll had an extra costume, hat and a piece of furniture, and on the reverse side of the dolls were directions for assemblage. The sets are not numbered and the number of pieces of furniture are unknown.

McLaughlin Coffee, "Victorian Ladies," series. (chokers/necklaces) $18-20

McLaughlin Coffee, "Victorian Ladies," series. $18 as shown

McLaughlin Coffee, "Victorian Ladies," series. $15 as shown

McLaughlin Coffee,
"Victorian Ladies,"
series. $12 as shown

McLaughlin Coffee, "Victorian
Ladies," series. $12 as shown

McLaughlin Coffee,
"Victorian Ladies,"
series. $4-5 each

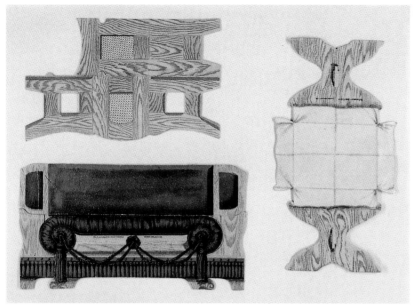

McLaughlin Coffee, "Victorian Ladies," furniture. $30 as shown

McLaughlin Coffee offered a series known as "The Standing Animals with Costumes." The animals came in pairs (Mr. and Mrs.), and each had separate underclothing, a suit or dress, a jacket or shawl (the wrap-a-round type), and a hat. The series included eight sets: Cat, Dog, Fox, Lion, Bovine, Monkey, Sheep, and Donkey.

Two humorous examples in the series are Mr. Donkey as a Dunce and Mrs. Donkey as a Teacher; Mr. Bull as a Butcher and Mrs. Cow as a Milkmaid. The numbered sets were printed by The Ketterlinus Lith. Co., Philadelphia.

McLaughlin Coffee, "Standing Animals With Costumes," Mr. Cat #1. $45 as shown

McLaughlin Coffee, Mrs. Cat #2. $45 as shown

McLaughlin Coffee, Mr. Dog
#3. $25 as shown

McLaughlin Coffee, Mrs.
Dog #4. $50

McLaughlin
Coffee, Mr. Fox #5.
$45 as shown

McLaughlin Coffee, Mrs. Fox
#6. $45 as shown

McLaughlin Coffee,
Mr. Lion #7. $50

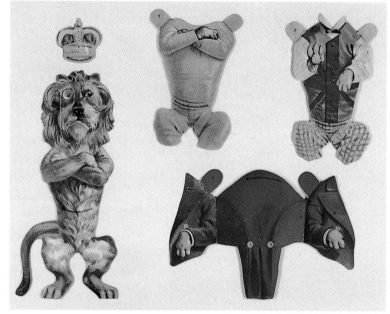

McLaughlin Coffee, Mrs. Lion #8.
$25 as shown

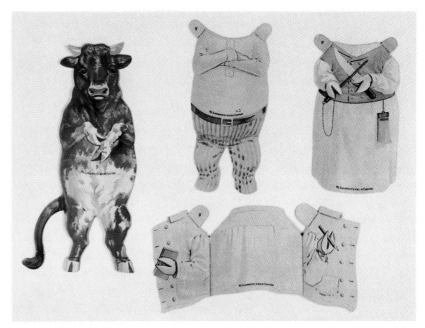

McLaughlin Coffee, Mr.
Bull #9. $45 as shown

McLaughlin Coffee, Mrs.
Cow #10. $25 as shown

McLaughlin Coffee,
Mr. Monkey #11. $45

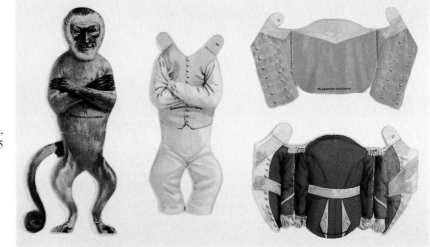

McLaughlin Coffee, Mrs. Monkey
#12. $20 as shown

McLaughlin Coffee, Mr.
Ram #13. $50

McLaughlin Coffee, Mrs. Ewe #14.
$45 as shown

McLaughlin Coffee, Mr.
Donkey #15. $45 as shown

McLaughlin Coffee, Mrs.
Donkey #16. $50

The series with folds on dolls and costumes are named "Sixteen Victorian Ladies,"
"Sixteen Young Ladies," and "Sixteen
Chubby Teenagers." All sets are numbered
and were printed by Koerner & Hayes, Buffalo, N. Y.

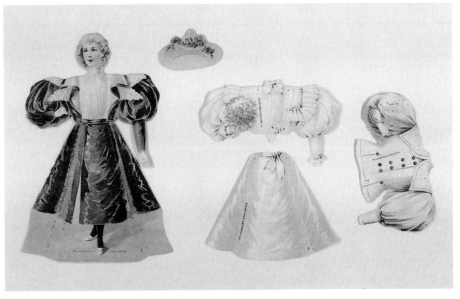

McLaughlin Coffee, "Sixteen
Young Ladies," series, #7. $18-20

McLaughlin Coffee, "Sixteen Young Ladies," series, #7. $12 as shown

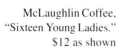

McLaughlin Coffee, "Sixteen Young Ladies." $18-20

McLaughlin Coffee, "Sixteen Young Ladies." $12 as shown

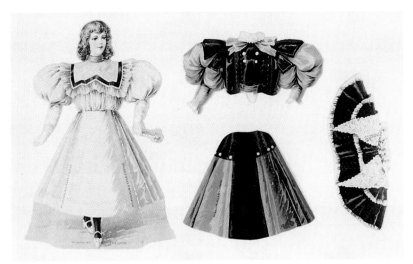

McLaughlin Coffee, "Sixteen
Young Ladies." $16-18 as shown

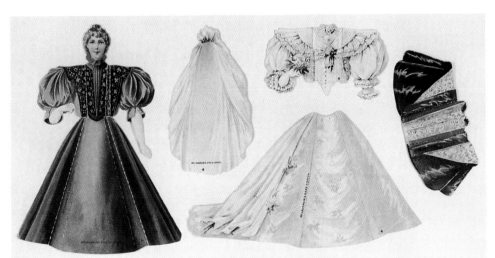

McLaughlin Coffee, "Sixteen
Victorian Ladies." $18-20

McLaughlin Coffee, "Sixteen
Victorian Ladies." $12 as shown

In the "Sixteen Young Ladies" there are two different doll sets using the number "seven." This indicates that there probably are two separate series for each of the sixteen sets. In the two sets numbered "seven," one young lady holds a flower but the second young lady does not. In the "Sixteen Victorian Ladies" some dolls hold a small gray card and others do not. In the "Sixteen Chubby Teenagers" some dolls hold a flower and others do not.

As minor design changes were made on the dolls, some costume pieces followed those changes, but other costume pieces did not. Thus, a collector will find the numbering system of costumes pieces confusing.

McLaughlin Coffee, "Sixteen Victorian Ladies." $16-18 as shown

McLaughlin Coffee, "Sixteen Chubby Teenagers." $18-20

McLaughlin Coffee, "Sixteen Chubby Teenagers." $16–18 as shown.

McLaughlin Coffee, "Sixteen Chubby
Teenagers." $12 as shown

McLaughlin Coffee,
costume pieces. $4 each

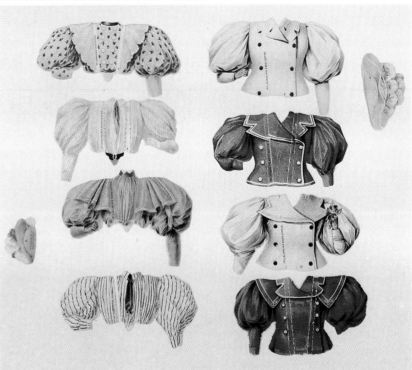

The "Victorian Ladies and Gentlemen" series consisted of eight wealthy society women and eight gentlemen with costumes having unusual side tabs which may help a collector to identify the set. The printers were Koerner & Hayes.

The great Irish immigration of the 1840s helped bring the Celtic observance of Halloween to the United States. The lighted jack-o-lantern was used as an early symbol trusted to keep witches from the door on All Hallows Eve.

In early times boys would tip over the outdoor privy or leave the barnyard gate open. Today, children dress in costumes and parade from door-to-door crying out, "Trick or Treat" where there is a porch light or lighted jack-o-lantern lighting the walk to a door.

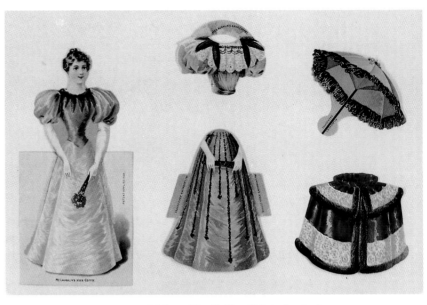

McLaughlin Coffee, "Victorian Ladies and Gentlemen," series. $18-20

McLaughlin Coffee, "Victorian Ladies and Gentlemen," series. $18 as shown

McLaughlin Coffee, "Victorian Ladies and Gentlemen," series. $18-20

McLaughlin Coffee, "Victorian Ladies and Gentlemen," series. $5-10 each

McLaughlin Coffee, "Victorian Ladies and Gentlemen," series. $18 as shown

McLaughlin Coffee, "Victorian Ladies and Gentlemen," series. $10 each

McLaughlin Coffee's "Cape" dolls, also printed by Koerner & Hayes, have the only known "Halloween" advertising doll of the insert cards. Close the cape, and the doll is a ghost with a jack-o-lantern head. Open the cape, and a little boy is revealed under the sheet holding the jack-o-lantern head on a stick. The "Cape" dolls are not numbered and the total number in the set is unknown.

McLaughlin Coffee, "Cape" doll, Halloween. (closed) Rare

McLaughlin Coffee, "Cape" doll, Halloween. (open)

McLaughlin Coffee, "Cape" dolls. $6-10 each

McLaughlin Coffee, "Cape" dolls. $6-10 each

The "Progressive" series, copyrighted 1894, were front and back dolls with a side fold, eight boys and eight girls. There was a change of face and occupation with each change of front and back costume.

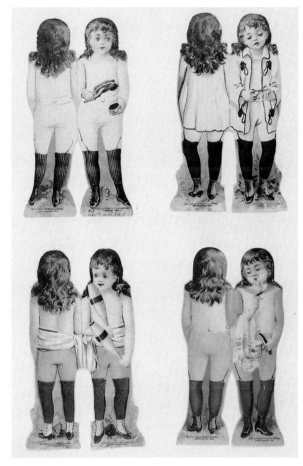

McLaughlin Coffee, "Progressive" series, girls. $10 each

McLaughlin Coffee, "Progressive" series, boys. $10 each

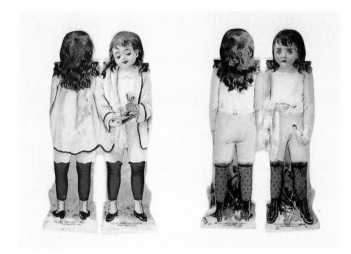

McLaughlin Coffee, "Progressive" series, boys. $10 each

McLaughlin Coffee, "Progressive" series, girls. $10 each

McLaughlin Coffee, "Progressive" series, girls' dresses. $8 each

McLaughlin Coffee, "Progressive" series, girls' dresses. $8 each

McLaughlin Coffee, "Progressive" series, girls' coats. $8 each

McLaughlin Coffee, "Progressive" series, girls' jackets. $8 each

McLaughlin Coffee, "Progressive" series, boys' suits. $8 each

McLaughlin Coffee, "Progressive" series, boys' coats. $8 each

McLaughlin Coffee, "Progressive" series, boys' suits. $8 each

McLaughlin Coffee, "Progressive" series, boys' coats. $8 each

Mechanical or Novelty dolls have a moving part. The pull out and the revolving disc are the most frequently used means of operating them. The McLaughlin issued die-cut mechanical dolls in color lithography, with directions for their assembly on the back of the doll. Each has two parts that will move when the lower end of a back piece is pulled.

For example, the butcher will move his eyes and chop meat, the Black child will open and shut his eyes and beat the drum, the cat will move his eyes and play the fiddle, and the woman will move her eyes and spank the boy. The number of mechanical dolls is unknown.

McLaughlin Coffee, Mechanical dolls. *Courtesy of Loretta Metzger Rieger.* $40 each

McLaughlin Coffee, Mechanical dolls. *Courtesy of Loretta Metzger Rieger.* $40 each

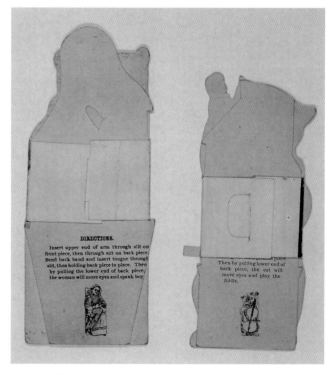

McLaughlin Coffee, Mechanical dolls, reversed. *Courtesy of Loretta Metzger Rieger.*

64

On the Fourth of July, the colors Red, White and Blue along with the Stars and Stripes Forever are always on parade in full regalia. To climax the Fourth of July celebrations, fireworks are used and displayed throughout the land.

In 1894 McLaughlin Coffee issued two dolls with fireworks. The boy with the American flag and cap gun is from the "Twelve Girls and Four Boys" series of front and back dolls with side folds. Miscellaneous items are portrayed around all of the dolls' feet in the set. The set was printed by J. Ottmann Lith. Co..

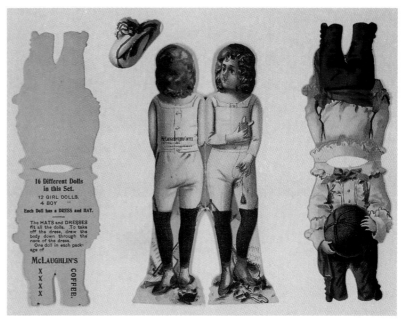

McLaughlin Coffee, "Twelve Girls and Four Boys." $10

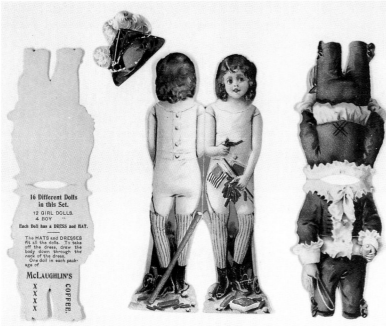

McLaughlin Coffee, "Twelve Girls and Four Boys," series, boy with the American flag and cap gun. $10-12

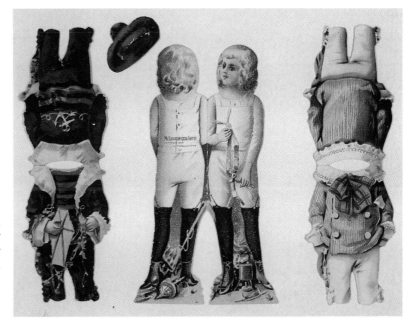

McLaughlin Coffee, "Twelve Girls and Four Boys." $10; $4 for extra costume.

McLaughlin Coffee, "Twelve Girls and Four Boys." $10; $4 for extra costume.

McLaughlin Coffee, "Twelve Girls and Four Boys." $10; $4 for extra costume.

McLaughlin Coffee, "Twelve Girls and Four Boys." $10

The boy with the fireworks is from the "Eight Girls and Eight Boys" series of front and back dolls. The boys have side folds at the shoulder, and the girls have side folds at the shoulder and hem line. The girls in this set are very hard to identify from the other small girls' sets.

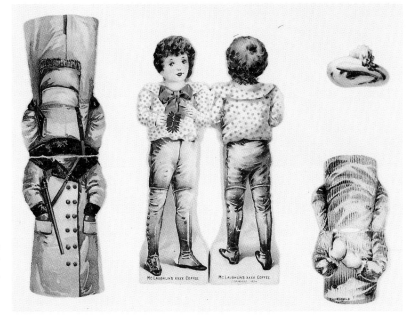

McLaughlin Coffee, "Eight Girls and Eight Boys," series, boy with fireworks. $10-12

McLaughlin Coffee, "Eight Girls and Eight Boys." $6 each

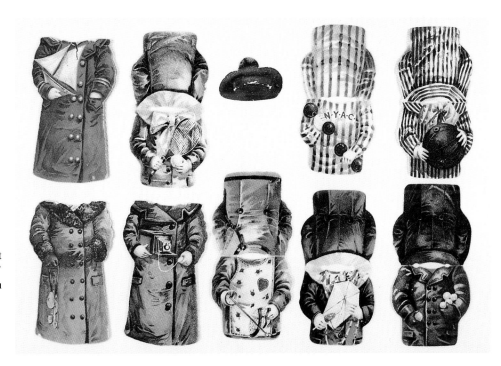

McLaughlin Coffee, "Eight Girls and Eight Boys," boys' clothing. $4 each

McLaughlin Coffee, "Eight
Girls and Eight Boys." $10; $4
for extra costume.

McLaughlin Coffee,
"Eight Girls and Eight
Boys." $10; $4 for extra
costume.

In a stand-up set, McLaughlin Coffee offered 23 different die-cut one-piece dolls in color lithography. Some of the dolls from this set were printed as cutout dolls for this company, and the set was also used as a stock set by many other companies for their advertisements. As an example, "Olympia" was used by the Wheeler & Wilson Sewing Machines.

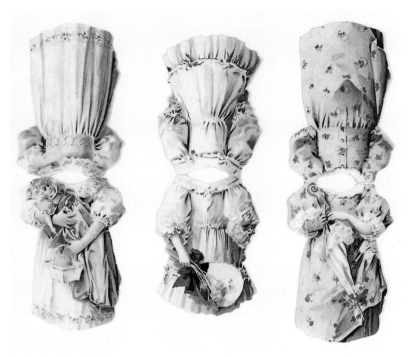

McLaughlin Coffee, "Twelve Girls and Four Boys," girls' costumes. $4 each

McLaughlin Coffee, Twenty-three stand-up Set, uncut and die-cut. $8-10 each

McLaughlin Coffee, Twenty-three stand-up Set, uncut and die-cuts. $8-10 each

In another stand-up set, the coffee company offered "Eight Boys and Eight Girls," shown as teens. Sometimes the dolls had a few small costume pieces and accessories. These dolls were printed in 1895 by Koerner & Hayes.

McLaughlin Coffee, "Eight Boys and Eight Girls," 1895, stand-up set. (teens) $8 each

McLaughlin Coffee, "Eight Boys and Eight Girls," stand-up set. (teens) $8 each

McLaughlin Coffee, "Eight Boys and Eight Girls," stand-up set. (teens) $8 each

A common set the company used was "The 4 Mammas, 4 Babies, 4 Girls, and 4 Boys." These were die-cut head-and-shoulder dolls in color lithography.

McLaughlin Coffee, "The 4 Mammas, 4 Babies, 4 Girls and 4 Boys." $8-10 each

In addition, there are numerous sets of front and back dolls with side folds at shoulder and lower side. These are all small children with one costume.

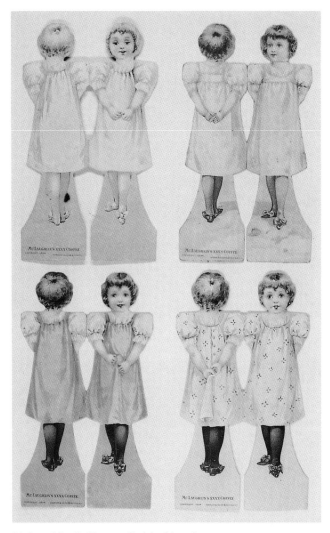

McLaughlin Coffee, small girls. $4 each

McLaughlin Coffee, small girls. $4 each

McLaughlin Coffee, small boys. $4 each

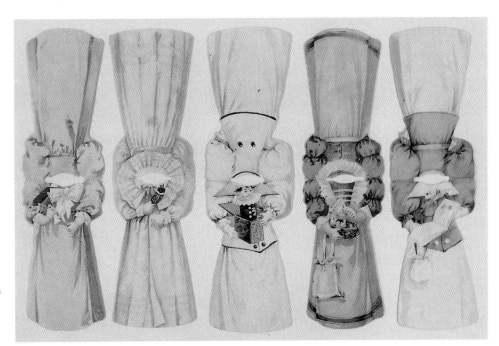

McLaughlin Coffee, small girls'
costumes. $4 each

An earlier printing of 16 front and back dolls as teens
with side folds bore the nototion "Copyright 1894 W. F.
McLaughlin & Co., Chicago." The front and back costumes
for these dolls have McLaughlin Coffee advertisements.

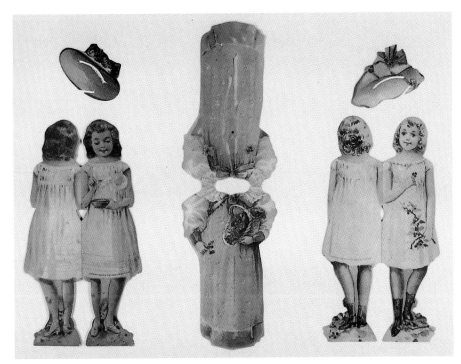

W. F. McLaughlin Coffee,
1894. $10; $5 for extra
doll.

Cordova Coffee, Dannemiller's and Co., Canton, Ohio

"Drink Cordova Coffee It Is The Best"

This company used die-cut "Brownies," which were printed in color lithography by Geo. S. Harris & Sons, of New York. Each doll in this set holds a different letter from the spelling of "Cordova Coffee". When the required number of Brownies were obtained to spell Cordova Coffee, Cordova mailed a fine gold ring in return for the Brownies, the ring size, and a two-cent stamp for postage. These Brownies are rare because many were turned in for that fine gold ring.

In addition, Cordova Coffee issued a cutout set of six amusing dolls in color lithography. One doll was placed in each pound package of the company's coffee. These were also mechanical dolls—for example, when the head-and-shoulder doll "Peter, Peter, Pumpkin Eater" is fitted to the body piece his head nods.

Cordova Coffee, "Peter, Peter, Pumpkin Eater." $6

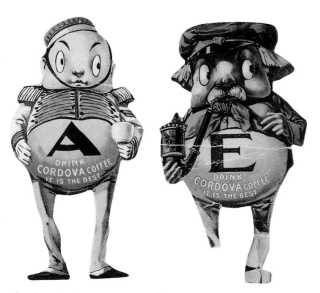

Cordova Coffee, "Brownies." $4 each as shown

Dannemiller's Royal Blend Coffee issued 12 die-cut "Liberty Dolls" in color lithography. A doll was packaged in each pound of coffee. The nations in this series are the United States, Canada, England, Ireland, France, Belgium, Russia, Italy, China, Japan, Serbia, and Brazil.

Each doll is dressed in an ethnic costume, and holds a carton of the company's coffee. The name of the country each doll represents is printed on the dolls. The P. B. Co., of Washington, D. C., was the printer.

Cordova Coffee, "Liberty Dolls." $6 each

The Old Reliable Coffee Company

The Old Reliable Coffee Company offered a cutout monkey, and a stock set named "Picture Painting Without Paints," which was a set also used by KIS-ME Gum.

"Always Buy Old Reliable Coffee"
"Always Good"

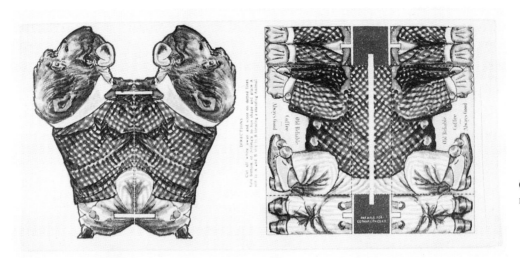

Old Reliable Coffee, monkey. $5

Dilworth's Coffee, Pittsburgh, Pa.

"Save the trade-mark on wrappers to procure a company of U.S. soldiers."

The paper soldiers this company offered were die-cut, in color lithography. The known pieces in this set include a very dignified U.S. Artillery Captain in his red-plumed hat, U.S. Marine Lieutenant, a mounted U.S. Cavalry Lieutenant, a mounted U.S. Cavalry Private, a U.S. Infantry Private, and a tent. The uniforms are from the late 19th to the early 20th century period.

Dilworth's Coffee, U. S. Cavalry Private. $10

A & P, The Great Atlantic & Pacific Tea Company

"200 Stores in U. S."

*"Our 8 o'clock Breakfast Coffee
is the epicure's delight,
And when used with our Condensed Milk,
It's just simply out of sight."*

The "Grandmother's Afternoon T Set" was issued by the A & P Tea Company to promote its sales. A die-cut set of ten head-and-shoulder dolls and a tea table in color lithography was given away at any store with a purchase of one pound of tea, baking powder, or spice, or two pounds of coffee.

Another die-cut set issued by this company was the head-and-shoulder dolls named "The Grandmother Set." These ten dolls were printed in color lithography by Armstrong & Co., Boston. The A & P trademark of "Grandmother," which the company used for a long time, is pictured on the reverse side of each doll's head. The trademark on "The Grandmother Set" is not printed as clearly as the trademark on the Grandmother's Afternoon T Set.

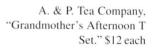

A. & P. Tea Company, "Grandmother's Afternoon T Set." $12 each

A. & P. Tea Company, advertisement.

A. & P. Tea Company, "Grand-mother Set." $10; $5 for extra dress.

Old Time Coffee, John Hoffmann & Sons Co., Milwaukee, Wisc.

"Save the Red Seals"

For ten seals and four cents in stamps, the company mailed a large fort. In addition, through the purchases of their coffee the company made available 29 different cards of military cutouts such as mounted cavalryman, sharpshooter, cannons etc.

The stock set was also issued as a premium for Silver Sea Coffee, The J. Henry Koenig Company, Cincinnati, and 27 cards for The American Bakery Co., St. Louis.

Favorite Coffee, Stephens & Widlar, Cleveland, Ohio

"Ask Your Grocer for Favorite Coffee"

The company issued a set of 12 die-cut head-and-shoulder dolls of different designs in color lithography. One doll was placed in each package of the company's coffee.

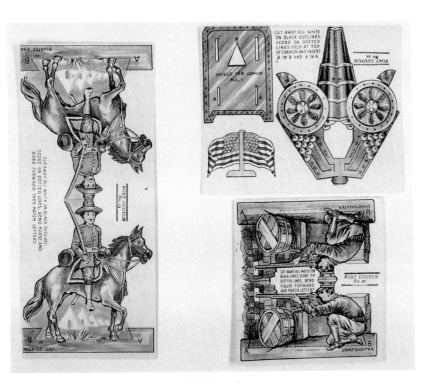

Old Time Coffee, soldiers etc. $10-12 each

Favorite Coffee. $12

Tea & Cocoa

Royal Garden Teas, The Bour Company

*"Unique among Coffees is
BOUR'S ROYAL GARDEN
The Kind with the Flavor"*

Royal Garden Teas offered two series of cutout paper doll post cards in color lithography. They were "Fairy Tales" and "Children From Many Lands."

These post cards of The Bour Company are similar to "The Fairy Tale and Children From Many Lands Dressing Series," published by Raphael Tuck & Sons, London & New York. The "Fairy Tales" post card #8 has a 1911 cancelled one-cent postage stamp.

Stollwerck's Breakfast Cocoa, Volkmann, Stollwerck & Co., New York

*"None Nicer
The Favorite of the Fastidious"*

The company provided a die-cut set of 16 statuettes, or head-and-shoulder dolls, in color lithography for six cents in postage stamps. The story of the appropriate fairy tale was printed on the inside of each costume, and the 16 dolls were listed: Little Bo-Peep, Ali Baba, Jack, Jill, Aladdin, Sleeping Beauty, Cinderella, Sinbad the Sailor, Rose Red, Snow White, Queen of Hearts, Jack the Giant-Killer, Little Red-Riding-Hood, Puss in Boots, Old Mother Hubbard, and Little Boy Blue. (Puss in Boots, Little Boy Blue, and Sinbad the Sailor are not pictured)

Stollwerck's Breakfast Cocoa: Red Riding Hood, Old Mother Hubbard, Jack and Jill. $12-14 each

Royal Garden Teas, post cards #7 and #5. $60 each

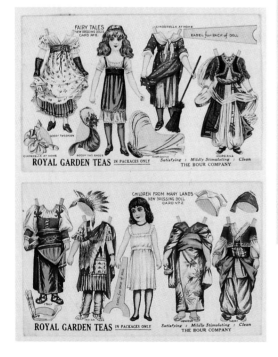

Stollwerck's Breakfast Cocoa: Cinderella, Little Bo-Peep, Queen of Hearts and Sleeping Beauty. $12-14 each

Royal Garden Teas, post cards #8 and #2. $60 each

Nestlé, a Swiss Cocoa company, issued cutout front-and-back dolls with costumes and hats in color lithography. In one example a Nestlé's Farine Lactée container is pictured with one of the doll's costumes. The paper sheet measures 7-3/4" x 8", and was printed by Moullot-Marseille, Geneva.

Stollwerck's Breakfast Cocoa: Rose Red, Ali Baba, Jack the Giant-Killer, Aladdin and Snow White. $12-14 each

W. H. Baker's Chocolate And Cocoa, Winchester, Va. & New York, City

"BEST"

The company mailed a die-cut set of six wrap-a-round dolls in color lithography for either a two-cent postage stamp or five Fleur De Lis trademarks cut from the labels of chocolate or cocoa.

The copyright date of 1897 appears on the front of the doll, and the company's advertisement is printed on the back.

Nestlé

*"La Joie Des Enfants
La Tranquillité
Des Parents"*

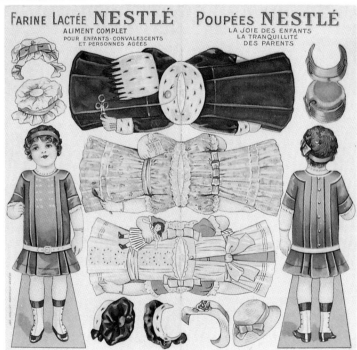

Nestlé. $20-25

W. H. Baker's Chocolate And Cocoa, wrap-a-round doll, 1897. $12

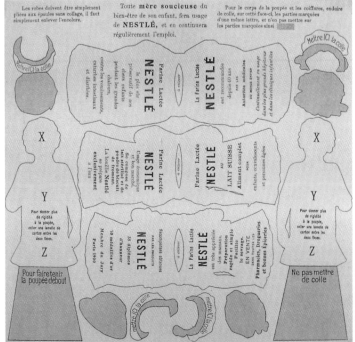

Nestlé.

Thread & Sewing Items

*"If The Child Who Receives This Doll,
Is Sent To The Store For Thread
She Should Ask For Clark's O.N.T.
Spool Cotton And See That She
Gets It."*

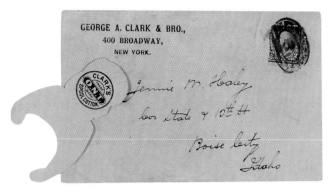

Clark's O.N.T. Spool Cotton, "Our New Thread", issued the finest of the trade card inserts.

Inspired by the social event of 1895, the wedding of Consuelo Vanderbilt and Charles Spencer-Churchill (9th Duke of Marlborough), George A. Clark & Brother of New York, makers of Clark's O.N.T. Spool Cotton, issued an advertising die-cut bridal set printed in color lithography. As in the high society wedding itself, the paper doll bride had a long, white bridal gown and veil trimmed with many silk ribbons and flowers; the men in the set were dressed in morning attire.

"The Dolls' Wedding Series" had 12 die-cut head-and-shoulder dolls, shown as children but dressed as adults. The dolls are approximately 5-1/4" in height. The set, which included the Bride, Groom, Minister, Father/Mother of bride and groom, Best Man, and four Bridesmaids, came through the mail in exchange for three two-cent postage stamps.

In recognition that the United States is a nation of immigrants, an ethnic set named "Dolls of All Nations" would have been mailed by the company in the 1890s for three two-cent postage stamps. The die-cut head-and-shoulder dolls for Clark's O.N.T. Spool Cotton were issued in color lithography by George A. Clark and Brother, New York.

Clark's O.N.T. Crochet Cotton, "Dolls of All Nations," envelope and a doll reversed.

Clark's O.N.T. Spool Cotton, "The Dolls' Wedding Series," Left to right: Row 1. (bottom) Father of the Groom, Mother of the Groom, Groom, Bride, Mother of the Bride, Father of the Bride, Bridesmaid with Forget-Me-Nots. Row 2. (top) Best Man, Minister, Bridesmaid with Daisies, Bridesmaid with Pansies, and Bridesmaid with Roses. $125-150

The set has eight ethnic groups, each represented by a boy and a girl dressed in their ethnic costumes: American, Scottish, German, Russian, Spanish, Italian, Turkish and Japanese.

"Dolls of All Nations," American girl & boy. $12-16 each

"Dolls of All Nations," German girl & boy. $12-16 each

"Dolls of All Nations," Russian girl & boy. $12-16 each

"Dolls of All Nations," Scotch girl & boy. $12-16 each

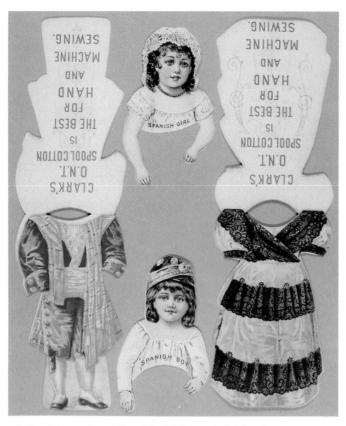

"Dolls of All Nations," Spanish girl & boy. $12-16 each

"Dolls of All Nations," Turkish girl & boy. $12-16 each

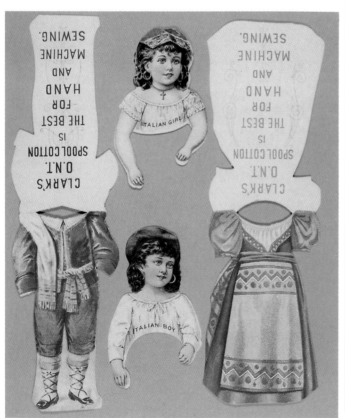

"Dolls of All Nations," Italian girl & boy. $12-16 each

"Dolls of All Nations," Japanese girl & boy. $12-16 each

In the 1700s in France a stately dance known as the "Minuet" became popular at the French court. It became equally popular when it was introduced in America, and in the 1890s Clark's O. N. T. Spool Cotton issued a beautiful set in color lithography of head-and-shoulder dolls named "The Minuet Series." It consisted of eleven die-cut pieces: four ladies, four gentlemen, one violinist, one piano player and a piano.

The four dancers from one "Minuet" set are pictured wearing costumes "Before the French Revolution." The dolls have powdered wigs, women are in waist pinchers, and men are in knee breeches similar to the way in which royalty and the upper classes dressed. The dolls in the second "Minuet" set are pictured in costumes "After the French Revolution." Wearing their hair in a natural style, women have loose ribbon ties around their waists, and the men are in long trousers.

Clark mailed the set for three two-cent postage stamps.

"The Minuet Series," piano player and violinist.

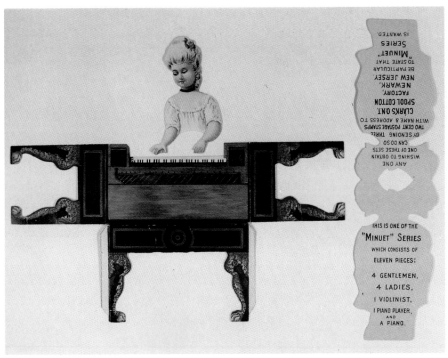

Clark's O.N.T. Spool Cotton, "The Minuet Series," The piano and a doll with costume piece reversed. Set: $200-250

"The Minuet Series," Minuet dancers.

"The Minuet Series," Minuet dancers.

"The Minuet Series," Minuet dancers.

"The Minuet Series," Minuet dancers.

Another colorful lithographic die-cut set issued by Clark was the 12 head-and-shoulder soldiers called "Soldier Boy Series." The set was mailed upon receipt of three two-cent postage stamps.

The series consisted of U. S. Infantry, Highlander (Scotland), U. S. Cadet, English, Swede, German, French, Austrian, Russian, Italian, Spanish, and Japanese.

Clark's O.N.T., "Double Dolls/Work and Play" Costumes. Left: #5 upper, #6 lower; Right: #7 upper, #8 lower. Heads: upper middle #5 & 6; Lower middle #7 & 8. $16-18 each

Clark's O.N.T. Spool Cotton, "Soldier Boy Series" $10-12 each

Clark's O.N.T., "Double Dolls/ Work and Play" Costumes. Left: #9 upper, #10 lower; Right: #11 upper, #12 lower. Heads: Upper middle #9 & 10; Lower middle #11 & 12. $16-18 each

Clark's O.N.T., "Double Dolls/ Work and Play" Costumes. Left: #1 upper,#2 lower; Right: #3 upper, #4 lower. Heads: upper middle #1, & 2; Lower middle #3, & 4. $16-18 each

"Double Dolls," known as "Work and Play," are 12 die-cut dolls issued by Clark's O. N. T. in color lithography. The dolls consist of shoulder-folded double dresses and top-folded double heads. The front view shows a little girl playing, while the reverse view shows another little girl working. Each side was given a separate number, and mailed to any address in exchange for three two-cent postage stamps.

Clark's O.N.T., "Double Dolls/Work and Play" Costumes. Left: #13 upper, #14 lower; Right: #15 upper, #16 lower. Heads: Upper middle #13 & 14; Lower middle #15 & 16. $16-18 each

Clark's O.N.T., "Double Dolls/Work and Play" Costumes. Left: #21 upper, #22 lower; Right: #23 upper, #24 lower. Heads: upper middle #21 & 22. $16-18 each

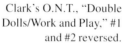

Clark's O.N.T., "Double Dolls/Work and Play," #1 and #2 reversed.

Clark's O.N.T., "Double Dolls/ Work and Play" Costumes. Left: #17 upper, #18 lower; Right: #19 upper, #20 lower. Heads: Upper middle #17 & 18. $16-18 each

Clark's O.N.T. "Dolls With Hats," copyrighted 1895, are die-cut front and back dolls in color lithography, with front and back costumes having a top-shoulder fold. The hats also have front and back views. There are four babies, four little girls, and four larger girls. Appearing at the corner base of each doll is the O.N.T. trademark, which pictures the bottom of a spool of thread. These dolls were mailed for three two-cent postage stamps.

Clark's O.N.T., "Dolls With Hats," 1895. $12 each.

Clark's O.N.T., "Dolls With Hats," $10; $5 for extra dress.

Clark's O. N. T. Thread was one of the companies which issued a common set known as "The 4 Mammas, 4 Babies, 4 Girls and 4 Boys."

The Clark Mile-End Spool Cotton Co., New York

"The Original Thread of America"
"The Black Spool"

Clark's O.N.T., "Dolls With Hats," $10

Clark's O.N.T., "The 4 Mammas, 4 Babies, 4 Girls and 4 Boys." $8-10 each

In 1896 the company issued a die-cut set of 12 animals, in color lithography. Two animals in this set were a polar bear and a hippopotamus, which were made to stand-up by attaching the legs of the smaller piece to the larger piece. The set cost three two-cent postage stamps.

Clark Mile-End Spool Cotton, animals. $4 each

J. & P. Coats

J.& P. Coats' "Ten Dolls With Hats." $16-18 each

*"Spool Cotton and Crochet Cotton
Is The Best For Machine And Hand
Ask Your Dealer For It."*

J. & P. Coats' Spool & Crochet Cottons offered two different die-cut sets of five paper dolls in color lithography. These dolls were meant as a child's plaything, but more importantly as an advertisement for the company's thread.

The dealer gave the customer a doll set which the company provided free of charge to purchasers of their thread. The set shows the doll holding an object, and the doll's costume has the same object but it is pictured differently.

J.& P. Coats' Spool Cotton, a doll's set reversed, and an envelope.

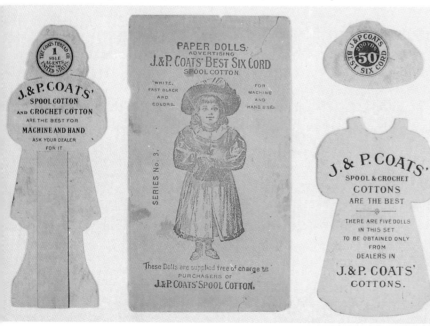

J.& P. Coats' "Ten Dolls With Hats." $16-18 each

J.& P. Coats' "Ten Dolls With
Hats." $16-18 each

J.& P. Coats' "Ten Dolls With Hats." $16-18 each

J.& P. Coats' "Ten Dolls With
Hats." $16-18 each

J. & P. Coats also offered a "Mechanical or Novelty" series of five die-cut paper dolls. Each had three revolving heads, and when the doll was reversed, another three revolving heads, with reversed costumes, and hats. The dolls were available from a J. & P. Coats dealer when a purchase was made for Spool and Crochet Cotton.

J. & P. Coats—Clark's O. N. T.

"The Two Great Names In Thread"

In 1930 and 1931, The Spool Cotton Company, parent company to Coats and Clark, issued two sets of John Martin's spool cutouts in color fast-print, a photo chemical-process which puts an image directly onto the printing plate, and through the use of a halftone screen the picture is broken up into uniformly sized dots, combining photography and lithography.

J. & P. Coats' "Mechanical or Novelty" series. $40-45

J. & P. Coats' "Mechanical or Novelty" series. $40-45

J. & P. Coats' "Mechanical or Novelty" doll showing two of three heads. $25

The company's "School Pets" set included Kitty Cat, Puppy Dog, Bob Bunny, Hal Horse, Clara Cow and Pete Pig. The second set, "School Zoo" included The Fox, Bear, Zebra, Lion, Elephant and Hippo.

TEDDY BEAR SAYS
With your sharp scissors cut me out carefully along the fine dotted lines.
Now, get a Spool of the right size to fit me. Spread glue carefully on both ends of the Spool, allowing it to harden a little; then stick my head on one end of the Spool and my tail end on the other.
There, you have me standing up for you as a nice BEAR should do.

J. & P. Coats' & Clark's O.N.T., "Spool Pets/Spool Zoo" (envelope). $4 each

Both sets of six animals each were obtained by sending in the appropriate postage, four cents in stamps for the "Spool Pets" and five cents in stamps for the "Spool Zoo," or by collecting one animal on a card in each package of J. & P. Coats' Bias Trim.

Coats' & Clark's, "School Pets," 1930. $4 each

Coats' & Clark's, "School Zoo," 1931. $4 each

J. P. Coats Mending Floss, The Spool Cotton Co., New York

DOLLY SAYS

Please, oh! please make me
 a dress
Or I must stay in bed,
Be sure and sew it carefully
With J. P. COATS
Thread.

The cutout doll, Dolly, in color fast-print on a paper sheet measuring 3-7/8" x 1-5/8," came packaged in a box of the company's mending floss. The advertisement on the back of the doll says, "Send four cents in stamps for twenty-four Hot Iron Patterns to embroider dolly's dress." Presumably, the 24 iron-on patterns are for a daughter's dress and not for Dolly.

J. & P. Coats' Mending Floss, Dolly. $12-14 (box)

Merrick's Spool Cotton, Merrick Thread Co., Chicago

"The Best For Hand
And Machine Sewing
Try It."

The company offered an ethnic die-cut stock set of 16 head-and-shoulder dolls, in color lithography, named "Native Costumes and National Emblems." The names of the countries the dolls represented were printed on the bottom edge of each costume piece.

By sending three two-cent postage stamps to the company the complete set would be mailed. This stock set was also used for advertisements of other companies, such as Pozzoni's Pharmacal Co., Doll Soap, and Sarica Coffee.

Another series which Merrick's Spool Cotton used was a die-cut stock set of 16 head-and-shoulder dolls, in color lithography. Buttermilk Toilet Soap Company also used the set for their advertisements.

The F-A Quality Family, F-A Quality

"A Word To Mother: these cut-out dolls serve two purposes; to amuse the children and to give you style suggestions designed by experts."

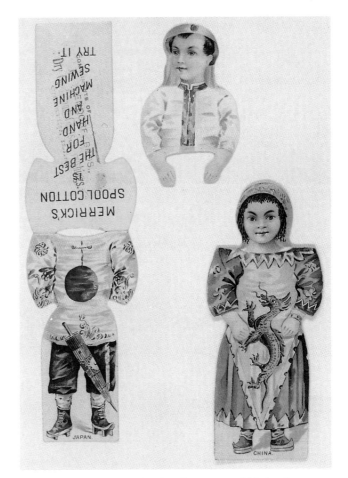

Merrick's Spool Cotton, "Native Costumes and National Emblems," Japan and China. $10-12 each

The paper doll, Betty, in color fast-print, has the family members, Mother and Buddy Sister represented as dolls on cutout sheets for F-A Quality Bias Tape. The dolls came packaged with the Bias Tape.

Merrick's Spool Cotton. $8-10

The F-A Quality Family. (Betty) $20

S. H. & M. Bias Velveteen Skirt Bindings, The S. H. & M. Co., New York

"See that the famous trade mark S. H. & M., is on every bolt of Bias Velveteen Binding you buy and – take no other."

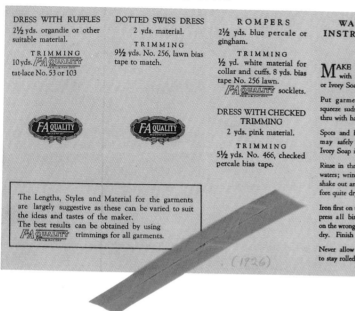

DRESS WITH RUFFLES	DOTTED SWISS DRESS	ROMPERS	WASHING INSTRUCTIONS
2½ yds. organdie or other suitable material.	2 yds. material.	2½ yds. blue percale or gingham.	MAKE a lukewarm suds with Ivory Soap Flakes or Ivory Soap.
TRIMMING 10 yds. *FA QUALITY* tat-lace No. 53 or 103	TRIMMING 9½ yds. No. 256, lawn bias tape to match.	TRIMMING ½ yd. white material for collar and cuffs. 8 yds. bias tape No. 256 lawn. *FA QUALITY* socklets.	Put garments in suds and squeeze sudsy water thru and thru with hands.
		DRESS WITH CHECKED TRIMMING 2 yds. pink material.	Spots and badly soiled places may safely be rubbed using Ivory Soap if necessary.
		TRIMMING 5½ yds. No. 466, checked percale bias tape.	Rinse in three clear lukewarm waters; wring; roll in a towel, shake out and hang. Iron before quite dry.

The Lengths, Styles and Material for the garments are largely suggestive as these can be varied to suit the ideas and tastes of the maker.
The best results can be obtained by using *FA QUALITY* trimmings for all garments.

Iron first on the right side, then press all bindings and seams on the wrong side, until thoroly dry. Finish on the right side.

Never allow colored materials to stay rolled when damp.

(1926)

The F-A Quality, reversed.

S. H. & M. Company. $20

There were three die-cut head-and-shoulder ladies, 8 3/4" inches in height and printed in color lithography by Sackett & Wilhelms Lithography Co., New York. A complete set was exchanged upon receipt of five two-cent postage stamps. The company's advertisements were only printed on the costumes.

World Fairs and Expositions feature exhibitions from nations around the world displaying the best of their products.

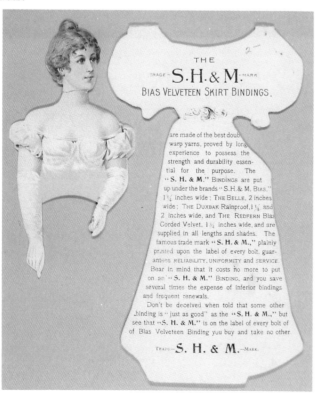

THE TRADE **S.H.& M.** MARK
BIAS VELVETEEN SKIRT BINDINGS.

are made of the best double warp yarns, proved by long experience to possess the strength and durability essential for the purpose. The "S. H. & M." BINDINGS are put up under the brands "S.H.& M. BIAS," 1½ inches wide; THE BELLE, 2 inches wide; THE DUXBAK Rainproof, 1½ and 2 inches wide, and THE REDFERN Bias Corded Velvet, 1½ inches wide, and are supplied in all lengths and shades. The famous trade mark "S. H. & M.," plainly printed upon the label of every bolt, guarantees RELIABILITY, UNIFORMITY and SERVICE. Bear in mind that it costs no more to put on an "S. H. & M." Binding, and you save several times the expense of inferior bindings and frequent renewals.

Don't be deceived when told that some other binding is "just as good" as the "S. H. & M.," but see that "S. H. & M." is on the label of every bolt of of Bias Velveteen Binding you buy and take no other.

TRADE **S. H. & M.** MARK

S. H. & M. Company, reversed.

S. H. & M. Company. $12 as shown

The Willimantic Thread Co.

"Willimantic Thread Highest Awards at N. O. Exhibition 1885."
"Willimantic Thread Highest Awards at Columbian Exposition 1893."

The Willimantic Thread Company issued four sheets (5-3/4" x 6-1/4") of cutout dolls, two boys and two girls, in color lithography.

The advertisements were printed on the back of the dolls and on each major piece of the costumes, so that when the pieces were cut the advertising would not be lost.

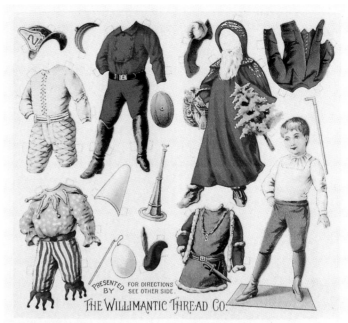

The Willimantic Thread Company. $50

The Willimantic Thread Company. $50

The Willimantic Thread, reversed: Columbian Exposition 1893.

The advertisement for the New Orleans Exhibition of 1885 is on the reverse sides of the girl with the doll and the boy with the hobby horse. The Columbian Exposition of 1893 is on the reverse sides of the girl with the lamb and the boy with the horn.

The Willimantic Thread, reversed: New Orleans 1885 Exhibition.

The Willimantic Thread Company. $50

Barbour's Irish Flax Threads, The Barbour Bros. Co.,

New York

"The Strongest, Smoothest and Best Linen Thread in the World."

In 1895 this company offered, in color lithography, a die-cut set of 12 dolls for three two-cent postage stamps. The Barbour's series consisted of six head-and-shoulder dolls—America, Ireland, Flower Girl, Little Buttercup, China, and Japan. The series also included six stand-up dolls—Orange Blossoms, Grapes, Sailor 19th century, In the Days of Columbus, In the Days of George Washington, and a Page, 18th century.

Barbour's Irish Flax Threads, doll reversed, with leaflet.

Barbour's Irish Flax Threads: Flower Girl, America, Ireland. $12 each

Barbour's Irish Flax Threads: Japan, Little Buttercup, China. $12 each

Barbour's Irish Flax Threads: Orange Blossoms, Sailor 19th century, Grapes. $12 each

Barbour's Irish Flax Threads: In the Days of Columbus, In the Days of George Washington, and Page, 18th century. $12 each

Clothing Styles & Patterns

"The Best in the World"
"Satisfaction Guaranteed or Your Money Back"

The giant mail-order houses of Montgomery Ward & Co. and Sears, Roebuck & Co. were widely accepted by rural customers, especially for their ready-made clothing in the latest styles. Many a talented homemaker proficient on the sewing machine was able to purchase patterns or copy styles as pictured in the "wish book" catalogs.

Wheeler & Wilson Sewing Machines

"Turn drudgery into pastime."

"Olympia," shown sewing an American flag on her new Wheeler & Wilson ball bearing treadle sewing machine, is a one-piece die-cut stand-up doll in color lithography. Another series Wheeler & Wilson Sewing Machines issued consisted of die-cut head-and-shoulder dolls in color lithography, where the advertisements were printed only on the front of the dolls' costumes.

The New Home Sewing Machine Company offered a cutout head-and-shoulder doll with front and back views of a Victorian lady seated at her sewing machine. The paper sheet in color lithography, printed by the Forbes Company, measures 8-1/2" x 5". Directions for assembly and the company's advertisement appeared on the front.

At the turn of the twentieth century, Charles Dana Gibson (1867-1944), an American artist, created drawings of a typical American girl, the "Gibson Girl," which influenced the beginning of a new fashion trend for ladies. This "look" had a wasp waist, with wide, puffy sleeves and many ruffles. In 1905 fashion figures in the "Gibson Girl" style were published in the Sunday news supplements of the *Buffalo Sunday News* and *The Sunday Sun*, New York.

The Singer Fashion Series, Singer Sewing Machine Company

"Perfect-fitting Patterns"

An advertising paper doll bride in the "Gibson Girl" style was issued by the Singer Sewing Machine Company in 1905, and patterns for her costumes were available for ten cents each from the Economy Pattern Company.

"The Singer Sewing Machine Bride" was a 9" cutout doll with a bridal dress and veil, three additional costumes, and three hats, printed in color lithography.

Wheeler & Wilson Sewing Machines, doll shown sewing the American flag. $10-12

Wheeler & Wilson Sewing Machines. $8-10 each

"Singer Fashion Series," dress and suit. *Courtesy of Virginia A. Crossley.*

The New Home Sewing Machine Company. $40

Singer Sewing MachineCompany, "Singer Fashion Series," 1905, bride and bridal gown. *Courtesy of Virginia A. Crossley.* Set: $70

"Singer Fashion Series," uncut dress. $18

The advertisement on the reverse side of the doll sheet covered detailed instructions, materials used, and pattern sizes, but when the doll was cut most of the advertisement was lost.

In another set, Singer Sewing Machine Company offered a cutout doll of a young lady in color lithography. On the reverse side of the set each major piece had the following advertisement printed.

"My Dresses are All Made on the Latest Improved Singer."

"Singer Fashion Series," uncut sheet reversed, pictured with the shirt-waist dress #5. *Courtesy of Virginia A. Crossley.*

Singer Sewing Machine Company, girl and costumes. $15 as shown

The complete set included a doll, two costumes, two hats, parasol, pair of shoes (legs attached), and a few small accessories.

J.& P. Coats, New York

"When you go to the store for thread ask for Coats Spool Cotton and be sure to get it."

In the second decade of the twentieth century, America became involved in the Great War (World War I) in Europe.

Fashions for women during this time were showing more freedom of movement, and were appreciated by the many women who worked on the homefront.

J. & P. Coats' WWI Wedding Set: Left (front row) Bridesmaid, Bride, Groom, Bride's Father. Upper (back row) Mother of the Bride, Minister, and on the right, the Best Man. Set: $75-80

At this time J. & P. Coats offered an advertising die-cut set of seven dolls in color fast-print. The bride's father and the best man appeared in U. S. Army uniforms of W. W. I., while the bride, bridesmaid, and the bride's mother wore dresses with the new hemline above the ankle.

A complete set was obtainable from the Spool Cotton Co., N. Y., in exchange for six cents in postage stamps.

The American Colortype Company, Clifton, New Jersey, produced a set "The Patriotic Dressing Dolls," for the *Farm and Home* magazine in color fast-print to be used as an award for selling magazine subscriptions. The cutout set consisted of two dolls, a boy and a girl, each with five costumes, and the dolls varied in the sets.

The American Colortype Company printed the dolls separately in envelopes for their paper doll line and also as a stock set to other companies. As an example the dolls were used by Bond Bread, Deininger Bakery, Rochester, N. Y.

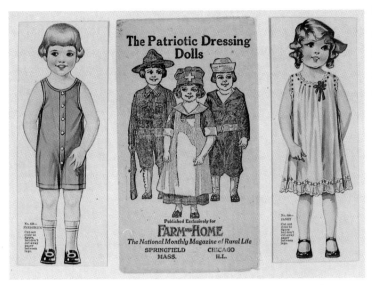

Farm And Home Magazine, "The Patriotic Dressing Dolls," and an envelope. (Frederick #623, Janet #608) Set: $35

"The Patriotic Dressing Dolls," Frederick's costumes, #847, #900.

"The Patriotic Dressing Dolls," Janet's costumes, #906, #903, #904.

"The Patriotic Dressing Dolls," Frederick's costumes, #823, #902.

"The Patriotic Dressing Dolls," Janet's costumes, #908, #907, and Frederick's costume, #901.

J. D. Larkin Company, The Thrifty Family, daughter Alice. $30

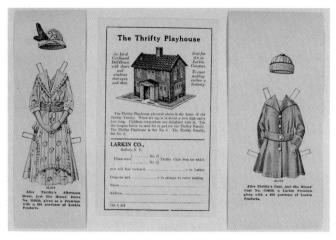

J. D. Larkin Co., The Thrifty Family's playhouse and costumes for Alice.

The La Salle & Koch Company, "Little Sister," 1918. (Elsie Dinsmore and Little Sister Dolls) $30-35

The Thrifty Family, J. D. Larkin Company, Buffalo, New York

"Of Course The Thriftys Are Stylishly Dressed."

The complete Thrifty Family consisted of Mr. and Mrs. B. Thrifty and their daughters, Alice and Mary. The cutout set of 19 pieces in color fast-print were mailed on request for four five-cent coupons, and two cents to pay for the cost of mailing, or four five-cent coupons attached to any order.

The "Wearing Apparel" in the wardrobe of the dolls are the exact copies of the actual items of apparel in the Larkin Spring and Summer Catalog, and were given as premiums with a $10 purchase.

In addition, the company offered a Thrifty Family's Playhouse for the dolls, which was mailed for twenty cents, in Larkin coupons and a two-cent stamp to cover mailing.

The La Salle & Koch Co., Toledo, Ohio

The La Salle & Koch Co., "Little Sister," reversed.

"Wear dresses just like your doll's"

In 1918, La Salle & Koch issued a 11-3/4" x 12" cutout sheet of an easel back doll, "Little Sister," in color fast-print from the advertising set named, "Elsie Dinsmore and Little Sister Dolls." The doll's costumes were examples of the department store's fine quality gingham dresses which they carried for small girls in sizes 2, 3, 4, 5 and 6. These dresses were priced from $2.25 to $3.75 each. The printer for the set was The Dandyline Co., Chicago.

Munsingwear, The Munsingwear Family, c.1920, cover. *Courtesy of Virginia A. Crossley.* Set: rare

The Munsingwear Company

The Munsingwear Company was a major producer of knitted underwear for adults and children.

The Munsingwear Family, c.1920, were cutout dolls in color lithography issued by the company to advertise the latest in their knit underwear for the family. The dolls came in one long strip with eight family members shown in their underwear: Grandfather, Grandmother, Father, Mother, Older Brother, Younger Brother, Older Sister and Younger Sister. Each of the adults had one costume and a hat, while the children had two costumes and two hats.

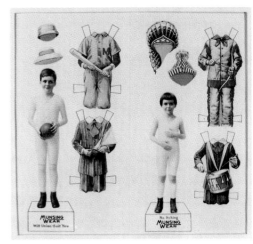

Munsingwear Family, Older Brother and Younger Brother. *Courtesy of Virginia A. Crossley.*

Munsingwear Family, Older Sister and Younger Sister. *Courtesy of Virginia A. Crossley.*

Munsingwear Family, Grandfather and Grandmother. *Courtesy of Virginia A. Crossley.*

The company distributed another cutout series in color fast-print named, "Miss Molly Munsing." The doll sheets were provided by the company to local stores for distribution and the retail stores could have their name and address printed at the top of each sheet, but when the doll was cut most of the advertisement was lost.

Munsingwear Family, Father and Mother. *Courtesy of Virginia A. Crossley.*

Munsingwear, "Miss Molly Munsing." $55

Munsingwear, Molly's costumes.

Duplex Corset, Bortree Mfg. Co., Jackson, Michigan and New York

"The Secret Out At Last Why Mrs. Brown Has Such A Perfect Figure."
"I WEAR THE DUPLEX CORSET"

The 1886 Victorian Lady cutout sheet (6-1/4" x 6-1/4") in color lithography used attached paper tabs to hold costumes on to the paper doll figure.

The company's advertisements were printed on the front and reverse sides of the doll, as well as on the reverse of the major costume pieces of the set. There were directions for cutting and standing the paper doll.

Kabo Corset/Ball's Waist

"All Corset Breakers Should Try The Kabo Corset"
"Try A Ball's Waist Once And You Will Never Wear Any Other Make, They Please Everybody."

Duplex Corset, trade card.
(closed) $20

Duplex Corset, Bortree Mfg. Co., Victorian lady, 1886. $75-85

Duplex Corset, Victorian lady, reversed.

Duplex Corset, trade card. (open)

The die-cut head-and-shoulder dolls are printed in chromolithography. The only advertisement on the front of the dolls was the attached slip they each carried in their right hand. (The Kabo Corset doll is missing her paper slip.) Advertisements appear on the backs and reverse sides of the dolls' costumes. The dolls were given to customers by store owners.

Kabo Corset/Ball's Waist. $18 each

Warner's Corsets and Warner's Brassieres

"A Style for Every Figure"

The cutout doll for Warner's Rust Proof Corset is in color fast-print. The advertisements for the company are printed on the back of the corset and dress. On the reverse side of the doll are the directions for dressing and her hat is labeled. A special message for Mother was printed on the back of the doll's trunk:

Warner's Corsets and Warner's Brassieres. $15

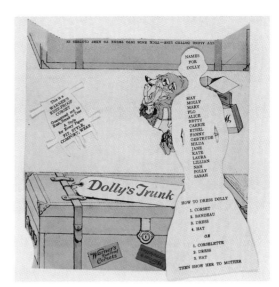

Warner's Doll's trunk, reversed.

Dr. Warner's Perfection Waists

"Made to fit all ages, from infants to adults"

The two dolls, a boy and a girl, were printed in color lithography in uncut card form. The uncut card of the boy measures 3-1/8" x 5-1/2".

Diamond Dyes, Wells, Richardson & Co., Burlington, Vt.

"Diamond Dyes Color Anything Any Color."
"It's Easy to Dye
With Diamond Dye."

In 1881 Diamond made 36 different colors for all types of fabrics and feathers.

Dr. Warner's Perfection Waists. $45 (uncut), $15 (cut)

Dr. Warner's Perfection Waists, reversed.

The complete die-cut set of six easel-back standing dolls and six extra dresses in color lithography were mailed free for two two-cent postage stamps. The company's advertisements were printed on the front and back of the set, and on the reverse side of each doll was a different satisfied customer's testimonial. The printer was J. Ottmann Lith., Co., N.Y.

Diamond Dyes, doll and two dresses, reversed.

Diamond Dyes, dolls and dresses. $16-18 each

Diamond Dyes, dolls and dresses. $16-18 each

Mayer Shoes, F. Mayer Boot & Shoe Company, Milwaukee

"'Special Merit' Seamless School Shoes Wear Like Iron."

The Mayer Shoe Company offered a series of paper doll post card advertisements, either sent through the mail or given over the counter by a shoe store owner.

The two small patriotic cutout dolls, Molly and John, are in color lithography and have front and back costumes. "Mayer's Custom Made" trademark appears on the front of each doll. The company's advertisement appeared on the addressed side of the post card, but when the card was cut some of the advertisement was lost.

Mayer Shoes, John. $8

Mayer Shoes, Molly. $8

Food & Confections

This group includes grocery products of all kinds, especially those in the grain classification. Advertising by cereal companies resulted in wheat cereal and hot cooked oatmeal becoming the breakfast of many families.

The American Cereal Company was one of the first that moved their oatmeal from the "cracker barrel" into packages, and later into the ready-to-eat packages of dry cereals.

Even in the 1890s, breakfast food makers competed for the "small fry's" favor by giving paper dolls and paper toys as premiums.

Brittle Bits, The American Cereal Co., Chicago

"The Heart of Grain"
COOKED READY FOR USE

"Should Brittle Bits lose its crispness through exposure, dry in slow oven," was the advice given in the company's advertisement.

"Little Miss Brittle Bits," 1901, was a die-cut doll, 15-3/4" in height, printed in color lithography, with four dresses and four hats. The doll's name, the company, the copyright date and the printer's name, Forbes of Boston, are on the front of the doll, and the company's advertisement appears only on the back of the doll. As stated on the envelope the doll sold for 50 cents.

Friends Oats, Muscatine Oat Meal Co., Muscatine, Iowa

"Does Thee Eat Friends' Oats"

In 1879, Friends Oats began doing business by the barrel with a capacity of sixty barrels a day. By 1900, the two-pound package of Friends Oats revolutionized the business. At this time, the packaging department had grown to a capacity of 60,000 packages every 24 hours, and the department employed 240 employees.

Brittle Bits, "Little Miss Brittle Bits," 1901. Set: rare

Brittle Bits, "Little Miss Brittle Bits," party dress.

Brittle Bits, "Little Miss Brittle Bits," golf costume.

Brittle Bits, "Little Miss Brittle Bits," jacket.

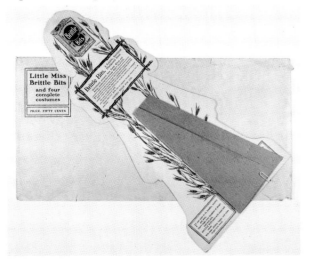

Brittle Bits, The American Cereal Co., "Little Miss Brittle Bits," reversed on envelope.

The little girl pictured on the box of Friends Oats was Maude Well Sawyer, daughter of J. P. Sawyer, General Manager of the company.

The die-cut wrap-a-round dolls in color lithography were from a set of seven dolls issued by the company. The company mailed the set for six cents in postage stamps.

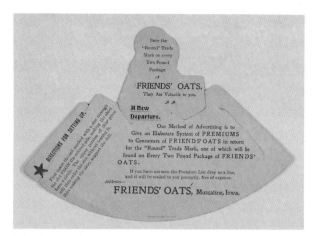

Friends Oats, doll reversed

Friends Oats, Muscatine Oat Meal Company. $20

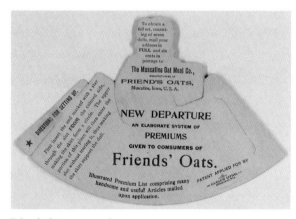

Friends Oats, reversed.

Friends Oats. $15

Germea

*"FOR BREAKFAST
The True Health Food"*

The company offered a cutout doll on a 3-1/8" x 5-1/4" card, with two dresses and a hat, in color lithography. On the reverse side of the card were five recipes for using Germea, and directions for cutting the doll. The Donaldson Brothers, New York, were the printers for the set.

Friends Oats. $20

Germea. $35

108

Germea, reversed for recipes.

Washington CRISPS, United Cereal Mills, Quincy, Illinois

"Toasted Corn Flakes"

In 1917, the company produced a "Mother Gooseland" series of cutout dolls. There were 51 different characters, a different character in every 51 packages of Washington CRISPS.

The 3" x 5-1/2" card of Cinderella and the Prince was printed in color lithography. In addition, the ground plan of "Mother Gooseland" would be mailed for four cents in postage stamps.

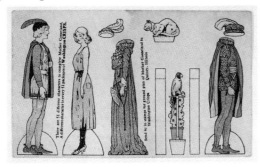

Washington Crisps, United Cereal Mills, "Mother Gooseland" series, Cinderella & Prince. $25

Victor Toy Oats issued a set of paper soldiers, in color lithography, consisting of an American infantry officer and men in dress blues, as members of "A Miniature Army" packed in Victor Toy Oats. The die-cut soldiers have wrap-a-round stands and are wearing the U. S. Army uniforms of the early twentieth century.

Victor Toy Oats, soldiers and envelope. Set: $90

Victor Toy Oats, soldiers.

Washburn Crosby's Gold Medal Flour, Washburn Crosby Co., Minneapolis, Minn.

"Superlative Flour Leads The World."

This is a common die-cut set known as "The 4 Mammas, 4 Babies, 4 Girls, and 4 Boys," and consisted of 16 head-and-shoulder dolls in color lithography. One doll was packaged in each sack of Gold Medal Flour.

Washburn Crosby's Gold Medal Flour, "The 4 Mammas, 4 Babies, 4 Girls and 4 Boys." $8-10 each

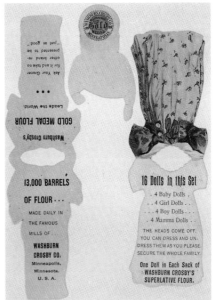

Washburn Crosby's Gold Medal Flour, doll reversed for advertisement.

109

Pillsbury's Best Flour, Pillsbury-Washburn Flour Mills Co. Ltd., Minneapolis, Minn.

"Pillsbury's Best Is The Best."

In 1895 the company issued easel cutout dolls in color lithography. No pasting was required, as each piece when cut fitted properly upon the easel by following the numbers on each piece respectively. When the dolls were cut, most of the advertisements on the back of the sheets were lost.

Pillsbury's Best Flour, Pillsbury-Washburn Flour Mills Co., Japanese lady, 1895. $25-30

Pillsbury's Best Flour, Dutch girl, 1895. $8-10

Pillsbury's Best Flour, Victorian lady, 1895. $8-10

Aunt Jemima Pancake Flour, R. T. Davis Mill Company, St. Joseph, Missouri

"Three Staffs of Life: Wheat, Corn & Rice"

In the advertising paper doll field there is a beloved figure, Aunt Jemima, who appears on the box of a pancake ready-mix which bears her picture and name.

In 1893, Nancy Green, who first portrayed the Aunt Jemima image, made her debut in presiding over a pancake demonstration at the Chicago World's Fair. Portraying Aunt Jemima for the company became a lifetime roll for her.

Later the company offered a set of cutout dolls in color lithography depicting Aunt Jemima and her five children: Rastus, Dilsie, Abraham Lincoln, Zeb and Dinah. These dolls are known as the "Before and After Receipt" set. "Receipt" is an old variant of "recipe," and the "Before and After" refers to the fact that, after Aunt Jemima sold her pancake recipe, she and her family were able to dress better, a circumstance reflected in their doll costumes.

When the dolls are cut some of the advertising on the back of the dolls are lost.

Aunt Jemima Pancake Flour, R. T. Davis Mill Company, "Before and After Receipt," costumes for Aunt Jemima's set reversed. *Courtesy of Loretta Metzger Rieger.* Set: rare

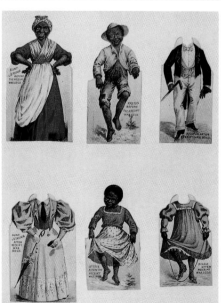

Aunt Jemima Pancake Flour, "Before and After Receipt," Aunt Jemima, and two children. *Courtesy of Loretta Metzger Rieger.*

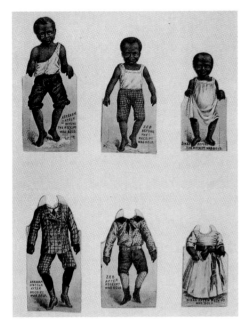

Aunt Jemima Pancake Flour, "Before and After Receipt," Aunt Jemima's three other children. *Courtesy of Loretta Metzger Rieger.*

Bond Bread, doll reversed, and an envelope.

The Quaker Oats Company in 1926 purchased the Aunt Jemima Mills, and in the 1930s a new Aunt Jemima, Anna Robinson, projected her magnetic smile upon the Aunt Jemima trademark. Portraying Aunt Jemima now became a lifetime roll for Anna Robinson as it had for Nancy Green.

Later in the Thirties the company issued a cutout doll, in the likeness of Anna Robinson, in color fast-print as she appeared on the carton of Aunt Jemima pancake mix. The doll is cardboard and her dress is of lightweight paper.

The Quaker Oats Company, Aunt Jemima, c.1930. *Courtesy of Loretta Metzger Rieger.* $20

Bond Bread, doll and dress. Set: $20 (envelope)

Bond Bread, Deininger Bakery, Rochester, N. Y.

*"DELICIOUS
The Best Bread Made"*

A different cutout set in color fast-print, consisting of one doll, three dresses, and three hats, was given away every day with each loaf of Bond Bread.

The advertisement for Bond Bread appeared on the back of the doll and on the envelope. The American Colortype Company, Clifton, New Jersey, printed the dolls.

Bond Bread, doll's two dresses.

Butter-Nut and Mother's Bread

"Greiner's Bread Is Worth Asking For"

A series of 24 cutout stand-up dolls was issued in color fast-print by the company. A different doll was given each day while the stock lasted, with a wrapped loaf of bread. The doll shown representing Italy has the copyright L. S. Evans.

Eatmore Bread

The Purity Baking Company, Ashtabula, Ohio and Erie Baking Company, Erie, Pennsylvania were local bread companies for Eatmore Bread. These local companies packaged in their wrapped loaves of Eatmore Bread a set of cutout dolls named the "Dressing Dolls" in color fast-print with one doll, dress, and a hat.

The American Colortype Co., Chicago, supplied the cutout dolls to different companies to advertise different lines of bread. For example, Butter-Nut Bread issued the "Dressing Dolls" in their wrapped loaves of bread.

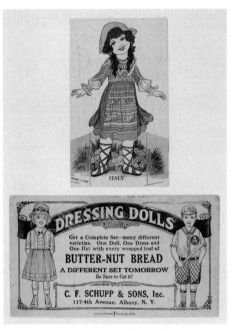

Butter-Nut and Mother's Bread. $8-10

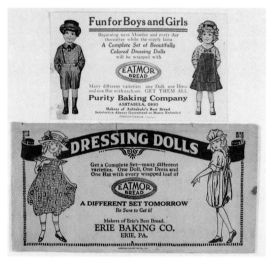

Eatmor Bread, advertisement and envelope. $8

Eatmor Bread, maid. $10

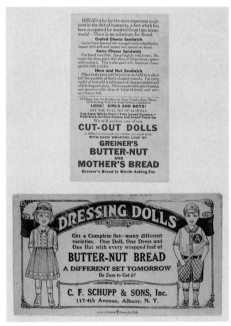

Butter-Nut and Mother's Bread, doll reversed.

Eatmor Bread, lady. $8 as shown

Sunshine Biscuits, Loose-Wiles Biscuit Co.

The die-cut doll on cardboard in color fast-print was offered by Loose-Wiles Biscuit Company, and was packaged in different products of Sunshine Biscuits. The costumes were: School Dress and Hat, Afternoon Dress and Hat, Birthday Party Dress and Hat, and a Coat and Tam-O'-Shanter.

K C Baking Powder, reversed: image of 1898 Gold Medal award.

Sunshine Biscuits. $10

Sunshine Biscuits, reversed.

K C and I C Baking Powder, Jaques Mfg. Company, Chicago

*"Purest and Best
Every Can Guaranteed"*

The K C and I C Baking Powders received the Gold Medal (Highest Award) at the Trans-Mississippi & International Exposition, at Omaha, Nebraska, in 1898.

The K C and I C die-cut wrap-a-round dolls are in color lithography and the only advertisement on the front of the dolls is the baking powder can they are holding. The reverse advertisement of each doll displays the gold medal which was received at the Omaha Exposition. The dolls were printed by The Gugler Litho. Co., Milwaukee.

I C Baking Powder, Gold Medal—1898 Trans-Mississippi & International Exposition, Omaha, Nebraska. $40

Pilgrim Baking Powder

"Once tried, always used."

The small embossed die-cut wrap-a-round doll in color lithography advertises Pilgrim Baking Powder. The doll was printed by the Eastern Speciality Mfg. Co., Boston. There is no advertisement on the back of the doll.

In the 1880s, Col. William F. Cody (1846-1917), known as "Buffalo Bill," brought his famous Wild West Show east. His show presented the "Romance of the West" to a contemporary generation. It was entertaining as well as a money-wise successful business endeavor for Bill Cody.

K C Baking Powder, Gold Medal—1898 Trans-Mississippi & International Exposition, Omaha, Nebraska. $40

Pilgrim Baking Powder. $10

113

Reid, Murdoch Baking Powder and Ground Spices, Reid, Murdoch & Company

"Absolutely Pure, Seldom Equalled, Never Excelled"

In 1895, Reid, Murdoch & Company, which sold baking powder and ground spices, issued five cutout cards (6" x 3-2/8") of easel dolls in color lithography, printed by Forbes Lith., Co., Boston. 50 different costumes could be made by varying combination pieces of the set. The set was named "Gibson's Wild West Dolls," and the doll "Washakie" represents a Native American. The company offered another five-card easel cutout set in color lithography called the "Gibson's Girls." The set had over 200 different fashionable costumes which were made by varying pieces of the set.

Anvil Brand Soda, A. J. Howell, New York City

"The Best for Bread, Cakes and all kinds of Pastry"

Anvil Brand Soda used one of the first issues of the common set known as "The Mammas, Babies, Girls, and Boys." In this series of 12 dolls some of the boys are shown wearing skirts like some young boys wore in the 1890s.

A complete set of die-cut head-and-shoulder dolls, in color lithography, could be obtained from the company by sending six large anvils cut from three large packages of Anvil Brand Soda.

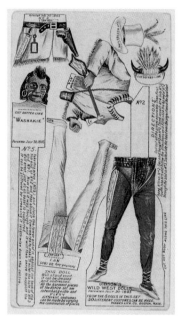

Reid, Murdoch Baking Powder, Indian, 1895. $25

Anvil Brand Soda, "The Mammas, Babies, Girls, and Boys," a doll with another costume reversed.

Reid, Murdoch Baking Powder, "Minnie", 1895. $25

Reid, Murdoch Baking Powder, reversed.

Anvil Brand Soda, mammas. $8-10 each

Anvil Brand Soda, babies. $8-10 each

Anvil Brand Soda, girl. $8-10

Anvil Brand Soda, girls. $8-10 each

Anvil Brand Soda, boys. $8-10 each

None Such New England Mince Meat, Merrill-Soule Co., Syracuse, N.Y.

"It pleases the young
It pleases the old
and every Grocer in the land is sold."

The company offered an ethnic set of five easel cutout dolls beautifully lithographed on cardboard. The dolls stand 8" in height, and each doll has two costumes, with hats and accessories, representing two ethnic groups: American/French, Russian/Spanish, Japanese/Chinese, Turkish/Indian, and German/Swiss. All easel pieces for the set are numbered for order of assembly. The advertisement on the front appears at the bottom of the body piece that bears the names of the two countries that the doll represents. The reverse advertisement appears on the body piece, and all the easel costume pieces are named for the country's costume they represent. Missing from the set are the German costume and the Swiss hat.

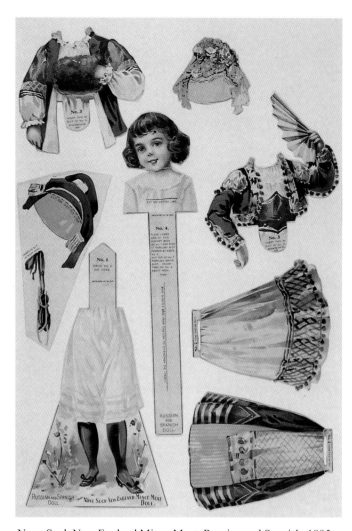

None Such New England Mince Meat, Russian and Spanish, 1895. $20

None Such New England Mince Meat, American and French, 1895. $20

None Such New England Mince Meat, Japanese and Chinese, 1895. $50 uncut

None Such New England Mince Meat, Turkish and Indian, 1895. $50 uncut

The dolls were sent by the company in exchange for five heads from the outside wrappers of the girl holding the pie, plus ten cents in silver or mailed free for twenty heads of the None Such New England Mince girl. The copyright is 1895, The Forbes Lith., Co., Boston.

None Such New England Mince Meat, advertisement for dolls. $18

New England Condensed Mince Meat, T. E. Dougherty, Chicago

*"The Fairy's Children
Who Ate The Fairy's Pie"*

None Such New England Mince Meat, German and Swiss, 1895. $10 as shown

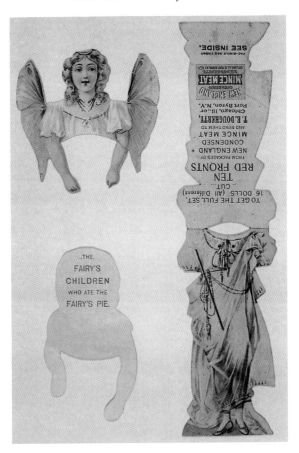

New England Condensed Mince Meat, fairy doll. $10-12   117

To receive the 16 die-cut head-and-shoulder dolls, in color lithography, one had to send the company ten "Red Fronts" from packages of New England Condensed Mince Meat. The Fairy doll was included in the set, and for another five "Red Fronts" one could also obtain the Fairy's Pie Booklet, which was a delightful Fairy story with a New England poem.

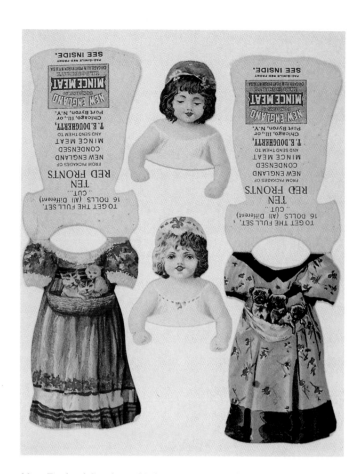

New England Condensed Mince Meat, girls. $10 each

New England Condensed Mince Meat, mamma and farmer. $10 each

New England Condensed Mince Meat, dolls in uniforms. $10 each

New England Condensed Mince Meat, girls. $10 each

Armour's Mince Meat, Armour and Company, Chicago

"The Veribest"

Phillip D. Armour, the Chicago meat-packer, knew that repetition in advertising encouraged customers to ask for certain brands.

As an advertising premium, Armour's Mince Meat issued a die-cut stand-up sailor or soldier in color lithography in every package of the company's mince meat. The American uniforms are of the Spanish-American War period.

Sinclair's "Fidelity" Hams, T. M. Sinclair & Co., Ltd., Cedar Rapids, Iowa

"Pork and Beef Packers"

In 1901, the Sinclair Company offered a die-cut stand-up doll with one costume, in color lithography. The "ugly" pig doll held a slab of "Fidelity" bacon, and his costume was a professor's garment with an abacus for counting. The advertisement for Sinclair appears on the front of the doll and on the back there is the company's hand-stamped advertisement.

New England Condensed Mince Meat, boys. $10 each

Sinclair's "Fidelity" Hams. $40

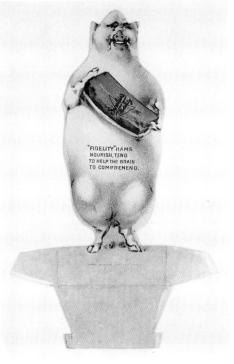

Armour's Mince Meat, soldier and a soldier reversed. $10-12 each

119

Swift's Premium Calendar, Swift and Company, Chicago

"Swift's 'Premium' Ham and Bacon"

The Swift's Calendar Dolls in color lithography were offered by the company for the calendar year 1917. The die-cut dolls are on heavy cardboard, with an easel-back for standing. The costumes and hats are on heavy die-cut paper:

Myrtle, a 20" doll, January, February, and March
Sylvia, a 19" doll, April, May, and June
Clarabel, a 19 1/2" doll, July, August, and September
Donald, an 18" doll, October, November and December

Swift's Premium Calendar, 1917, Sylvia's costume—October, November and December.

Swift's Premium Calendar, 1917, Sylvia—April, May and June. Set: $175

Swift's Premium Calendar, 1917, Sylvia's costume—July, August and September

Swift's Premium Calendar, 1917, Sylvia's costume— January, February, and March.

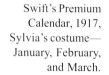

The three costumes of each doll completes the 1917 calendar year for each individual doll.

The advertisements on the back of Sylvia and her hats are for ham and bacon, and her costumes have advertising for other Swift's products.

Swift's Premium Calendar, 1917, Swift's Cotosuet Advertisement.

Burnham's Clam Chowder, Burnham Company, New York City

"A whole dinner in a can"

The company offered a set of five different dolls sent free on receipt of two red Diamond Trade Marks, cut from packages of certain Burnham's products. The Clam Chowder die-cut wrap-a-round doll is pictured as a black cook carrying a huge bowl of clam chowder. The printing company was David Weils Sons Co., New York.

Burham's Clam Chowder. $8 as shown

Epicure Ham and Boneless Bacon, Cortland Beef Company, Cortland, New York

*"My Papa and Mamma both say that
Epicure Hams and Boneless Bacon
Are the Best."*

The company's die-cut head-and-shoulder doll, in color lithography, is from a common stock set which many companies used for advertising. For example, Dr. R. V. Pierce, Buffalo, New York, used the same stock set for his advertisements. The advertising for the Cortland Beef Company appears on the back of the doll's costume.

In the late 1800s and early 1900s, a few companies began to give black advertising dolls as premiums. Black men and women were usually portrayed as a chef or cook and black children as young comedians.

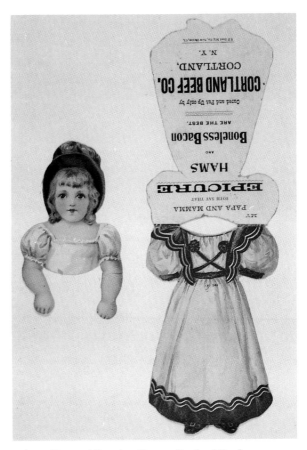

Epicure Ham and Boneless Bacon, Cortland Beef Company. $10

De Laval Cream Separators, The De Laval Separator Co., New York

*"Have Revolutionized Dairying
All Styles and Sizes
$50 to $800"*

The company offered a die-cut stand-up doll as a milk-maid with her cow, in color lithography.

Later the De Laval Company issued sets of the Ideal Milking Cow and Her Calf in fast-print, to be punched out. The card for the Brown Swiss Cow and Calf is 4-1/4" x 7".

De Laval Cream Separators, cow and milkmaid reversed.

De Laval Cream Separators. $10

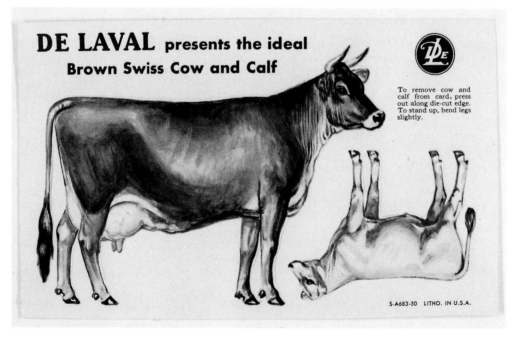

De Laval Cream Separators. $8

122

Shaker Salt Doll Book, The Diamond Crystal Salt Co., St. Clair, Mich.

"Send ten cents and your address"

The Shaker Doll Book, *Travels of the Shaker Salt Doll in the Royal Table Lands of the World*, was a combination of a study and a cutout doll book. The book was published in 1911 for the Diamond Crystal Salt Company and the book was received through the mail for the sum of ten cents.

For educational value, the set included verses describing the doll's travels and a short history of a child's life in each country visited by the Shaker Salt doll. The ethnic set represented seven Royal Table Lands of the World: England, Spain, Germany, Russia, Turkey, China and Japan. Each doll had an additional costume, and the Shaker Salt doll had two additional costumes. Her costumes included a coat where she holds a Shaker Salt box and a dress designed as a "salt shaker." The Shaker Salt trademark is positioned so that it remains on the back of all cut pieces.

Worcester Salt Bags, Worcester Salt Co., New York

*"Has no equal for
Table, Kitchen or Dairy."*

The Worcester's salt was for sale by grocers everywhere from Maine to California. The company issued 12 die-cut stand-up dolls, in color lithography, in two equal groups. One, the "Floral Group," consisted of six dolls, named Morning Glory, Iris, Carnation, Tulip, Water-Lilies and Sweet Pea, and the six dolls in the "Ethnic Group" were an American Indian, American, American Black, Irish, Dutch, and a Chinese.

The entire set was mailed anywhere for either six coupons from Worcester Salt Bags or one coupon and three two-cent postage stamps. The Worcester company's advertisement appeared only on the back of the dolls. These 12 dolls were also issued for Enameline Stove Polish as two sets.

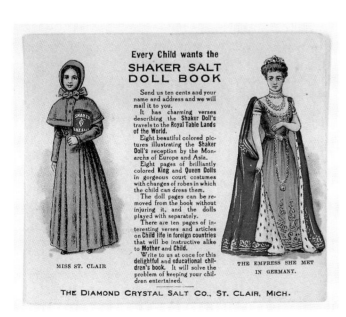

Shaker Salt Doll Book's Coupon. $12

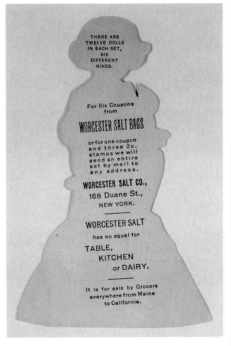

Worcester Salt Bags, dolls reversed.
(Nursery Rhymes/Floral Group)

Worcester Salt, "Floral Group," Morning Glory, Iris, and Carnation. $12-15 each

Another group for Worcester Salt was a "Nursery Rhyme" set of die-cut stand-up dolls in color lithography. The set included Little Miss Muffet, Little Jack Horner, Little Tommy Tucker, Little Bo-Peep, Little Boy Blue, and Mistress Mary. The company's advertisement appeared only on the back of the dolls.

Worcester Salt, "Nursery Rhymes," Little Miss Muffet, Little Jack Horner, and Little Tommy Tucker. $12 each

Worcester Salt, "Floral Group," Tulip, Water-Lilies, and Sweet Pea. $12-15 each

Worcester Salt, "Nursery Rhymes," Little Bo-Peep, Little Boy Blue, and Mistress Mary. $12 each

Virginia Dare Flavoring Extracts, Garrett & Company (Food Products) Brooklyn, N. Y.

*"Virginia Dare Double Strength Extracts
There are 21 flavors in all."*

Virginia Dare Flavoring Extracts offered a set of "Kiddie Kuts" in color fast-print. In the three cutout pieces, Virginia is shown coming home from the market, mixing her cake, and eating her cake at her tea table. Another piece shows Virginia baking. Advertisements are on both sides of each doll, and the advertisments on the back of the dolls were not lost in the cuttings.

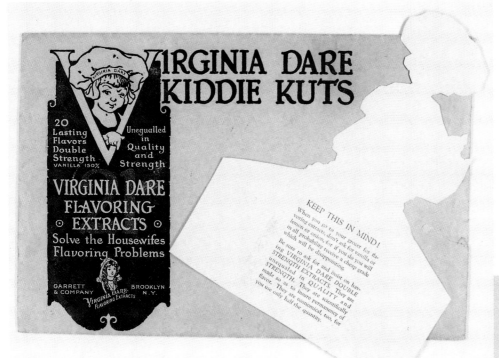

Virginia Dare Flavoring Extracts, doll reversed and an envelope.

Virginia Dare, coming home from the market.
Set: $18-20 as shown (envelope)

Virginia Dare, measuring her extract.

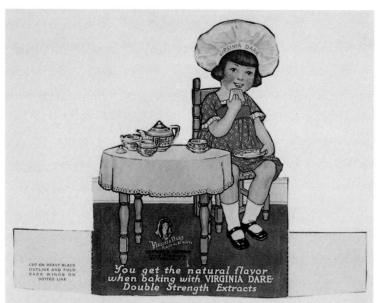

Virginia Dare, eating her cake.

Cake of Sugared Pop Corn, F. W. Rueckheim & Bro., Chicago

"The Dolls Are A Great Amusement For Children, Given Free With Each Cake Of Sugared Pop Corn"

The Rueckheim Company offered an early set of die-cut advertising dolls, 7-1/8" in height, in chromolithography. There were four dolls, each with a costume and hat. The company's advertisement appears only on the back of the dolls. One set is given free with each "Cake of Sugared Pop Corn."

Cake of Sugared Pop Corn, F. W. Rueckheim & Bro. $10-12 as shown

Flavoring Extracts, Foote and Jenks Manufacturers, Jackson, Michigan

"They are the Best"

The dolls are two humorous cats, with one biting his tail and the other smoking a pipe. The die-cut stand-ups in color lithography are from a stock set. The company rubber-stamped their advertising on the front of each doll in red, and used a purple color for their name on the back.

Foote and Jenks were manufacturers of perfumes and flavoring extracts, a combination not uncommon among early perfume manufacturing companies.

Flavoring Extracts, Foote and Jenks. $8 each

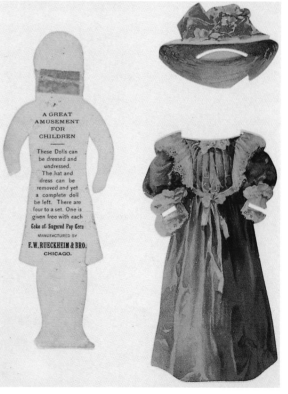

F. W. Rueckheim & Bro., doll reversed.

126

Adam's Pepsin Tutti Frutti Gum

"Aids Digestion"

Thomas Adams's Tutti Frutti gum was the first to be widely advertised in the late 1800s. The company issued a die-cut head-and-shoulder doll in color lithography. The advertisement was on the back of the doll's costume.

Adam's Pepsin Tutti Frutti Gum. $12

"KIS-ME" Chewing Gum, KIS-ME GUM CO., Louisville, Ky.

"Everybody's Favorite"

Jonathan P. Primley was an Elkhorn, Indiana, manufacturer and an advertising genius, who named his gum product KIS-ME in an attempt to capture the romance market. The brand was so successful that he named his concern the Kis-Me Gum Company. Later the company merged with American Chicle Company, the manufacturers of "Chicolettes."

A "Mother Goose" series of twelve die-cut head-and-shoulder dolls, in color lithography, were sent by the Kis-Me Gum Company on receipt of six cents in postage stamps and six "Kis-Me" gum wrappers.

The company's advertisement was printed on the back of the dolls' costume and the appropriate nursery rhyme was printed on the inside of the costume. The dolls in the set were not listed, but six dolls from the set are Peter, Peter, pumpkin eater, Little Bo-Peep, Little Jack Horner, Daffy-down dilly, Tom he was a piper's son, and Humpty-Dumpty. The dolls were printed by The Orcutt Co., Chicago.

KIS-ME Chewing Gum, "Mother Goose," series: Peter, Peter, Pumpkin Eater and Little Bo-Peep. $15-18 each

127

KIS-ME Chewing Gum, "Mother Goose," series: Little Jack Horner, and Daffy-Down Dilly. $15-18 each

"Picture Painting Without Paints", The American Chicle Co., (KIS-ME Gum Factory) Louisville, Ky.

"No Soiled Hands or Clothing only a Pair of Scissors Required."

The American Chicle Company offered a delightful children's cutout in four designs, in color lithography, with a glue backing that required only moistening when the dolls were assembled. The designs were: Blind Man's Buff, In Fancy Dress, Going to School, and Off to Town. The printer was Gotham Litho. Co., N. Y.

The company would mail one doll upon receipt of five Kis-Me Wrappers and two cents in postage stamps, or two dolls for four cents in stamps and five wrappers, or three dolls for five cents in stamps and five wrappers, or four dolls (the complete set) for six cents in stamps and five wrappers. The company's advertisement appeared on the background sheet as did the directions for assembly. The stock set was also used by Old Reliable Coffee.

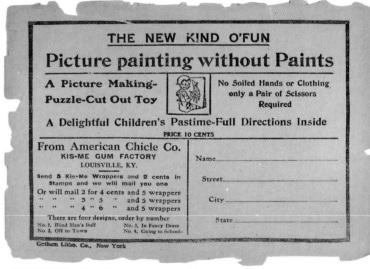

KIS-ME Chewing Gum, American Chicle Co., envelope for "Picture Painting Without Paints." $5

KIS-ME Chewing Gum, "Mother Goose:" series: Tom, He Was a Piper's Son, and Humpty-Dumpty. $15-18 each

KIS-ME Chewing Gum, American Chicle Co., Blind Man's Buff, Part I. $10

KIS-ME Chewing Gum, American Chicle Co., Blind Man's Buff, Part II. $10

KIS-ME Chewing Gum, American Chicle Co., In Fancy Dress, Part I. $10

KIS-ME Chewing Gum, American Chicle
Co., In Fancy Dress, Part II. $10

KIS-ME Chewing Gum,
American Chicle Co., Going to
School, Part I. $10

KIS-ME Chewing Gum, American Chicle
Co., Going to School, Part II. $10

KIS-ME Gum, American Chicle Co., (Old Reliable Coffee), Off to Town, Part I. $8-10

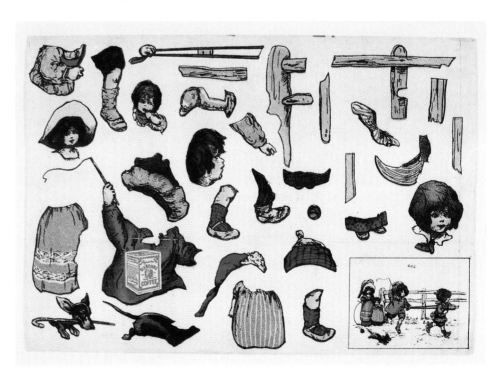

KIS-ME Gum, American Chicle Co., (Old Reliable Coffee), Off to Town, Part II. $8-10

Happy Family Candy

"One Doll with Every Stick of Candy"

This company's 16 head-and-shoulder dolls in color lithography were the common die-cut set of "The 4 Mammas, 4 Babies, 4 Girls, and 4 Boys." The company included a Black girl in the set as one of the dolls to be given with every stick of candy. The company's advertisement is only on the back of the dolls' costumes.

Happy Family Candy. $10-12

"Brownies" Chocolate Cream Drops, Hawley & Hoops, New York

*"A No. 1
TRY THEM"*

The Hawley and Hoops Company copyrighted the word "Brownies," on November 22, 1887. The 3-1/2" x 4" uncut card showing a Palmer Cox Brownie doll dressed as a sailor was issued for Brownies Chocolate Cream Drops. The lithographers were The Thomas and Wylie, Litho. Co., New York, 1892, by permission of Arnold Print Works, North Adams, Massachusetts.

Penny Chocolate Candies & Breakfast Cocoa, Hawley & Hoops, New York

*"Better Than Coffee or Tea For Everybody
Made of Pure Chocolate"*

The cocoa company produced chocolate "Penny Goods" for young children to purchase at the neighborhood corner store. The cutout sailor suit for a bear is in color lithography.

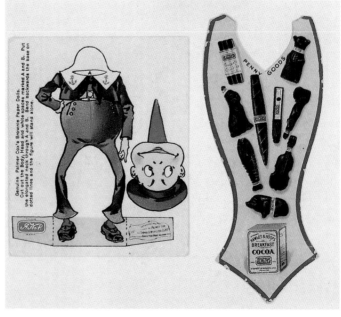

"Brownies" Chocolate Cream Drops, Hawley & Hoops Co. (Palmer Cox Brownie) $20-25 as shown

132

Zatek Cocoa, Pennsylvania Chocolate Co., Pittsburgh

"Sold Under A Money-back Guarantee"

In 1918 the company offered 14 stand-up dolls, in color fast-print, showing Miss Zatek and her Papoose. Each different cutout doll has a letter for the spelling of Zatek Chocolate. One stand-up doll was packaged in each cake of Zatek Milk Chocolate.

Zatek Cocoa, Pennsylvania Chocolate Co. $10 each

Zatek Cocoa, reversed.

Household

This category deals with the advertising dolls issued as premiums to help promote the many household products and similar items which the homemaker might need.

Enameline, J. L. Prescott & Co., New York

E very lady in the land
N ow has a Polish at her hand,
A nd thinks it better than a bar,
M ore quickly used, much better far.
E asy, clean, bright of shine,
L ovely, she says,
I n saving time.
N one was ever seen like
E NAMELINE.

Enameline, "Enameline College Colors," Princeton University, Illinois Wesleyan University, and Cornell University. $40 each

Enameline, "Enameline College Colors," Oberlin College, Yale University, and Harvard University. $40 each

Enameline, "Enameline College Colors," Bryn Mawr College, Wellesley College, and Vassar College. $40 each

Enameline, "the modern stove polish," offered several beautiful die-cut sets in color lithography.

Every college and university encourages its student body to root for the school in all of its activities. The set of "Enameline College Colors" consists of nine dolls representing different colleges, with their appropriate colors and college cheers. The dolls exemplify Oberlin College, Yale University, Harvard University, Princeton University, Illinois Wesleyan University, Cornell University, Bryn Mawr College, Wellesley College and Vassar College. They were mailed upon receipt of either three two-cent postage stamps or two two-cent postage stamps and three top labels from boxes of Enameline.

Enameline, "Enameline Flowers," Rose and Pansy. $18-20 each

Enameline, "Enameline Standing Animals," Goat, and "Enameline Flowers," Rose, reversed.

Enameline, "Enameline Flowers," Chrysanthemum and Poppy. $18-20 each

Enameline, "Enameline Flowers," Violet and Primrose. $18-20 each

Enameline, "Enameline Standing Animals," pig and monkey. $20 each

Enameline, "Enameline Standing Animals," goat and cat. $20 each

Enameline, "Enameline Standing Animals," dog and fox. $20 each

The "Enameline Flowers" set consists of six dolls, which are named Rose, Pansy, Poppy, Chrysanthemum, Violet and Primrose. A complete set was obtained by sending three two-cent postage stamps to the company.

*"The Modern Stove Polish
It's Up To Date."*

In the "Enameline Standing Animals" set there are six animals dressed-up and doing human's work. They are a cat, goat, dog, fox, monkey, and pig. A complete set was mailed for either three two-cent postage stamps, or two two-cent stamps and three top labels from boxes of Enameline.

*"Ready to use,
easily applied,
dustless, black and brilliant"*

Enameline issued two common sets of six die-cut stand-up dolls in color lithography, which were also used by Worcester Salt and local companies, such as Farrand Organs.

The "Enameline Ethnic Group" depicted an American Indian, American, American Black, Irish, Dutch and a Chinese. The Enameline advertisements appeared on the front and back of the dolls.

The "Floral Group" set depicted Morning Glory, Iris, Carnation, Tulip, Water-Lilies, and Sweet Pea. The Enameline advertisements appeared on the front and back of the dolls. Each set was mailed upon receipt of either two two-cent postage stamps or three one-cent postage stamps and three Enameline labels.

*"Enameline Is Never
Peddled"*

Enameline, "Enameline Ethnic Group," American Indian, American, and American Black. $15 each

Enameline, "Emameline Ethnic Group," Irish, Dutch, and Chinese. $15 each

137

Before 1900, the publishing company of Raphael Tuck & Sons, was well established in London, Paris, Berlin and New York. A few of the company's beautiful die-cut dolls in color lithography have been used to advertise other companies' products.

As an example, the doll "My Lady Betty" (artist Madge McDonald), Artistic Series 102, was used to advertise household ranges. The doll's three costumes and two hats are marked Artistic Series 101 and the advertising appears only on the hats in the set. A third hat was included in the set.

Another doll, "Winsome Winnie," Artistic Series 103, was also used to advertise household ranges. Her three costumes and three hats are marked Artistic Series 104 but only the hats have the marking "Buy Household Ranges." On the reverse side of each doll, as well as her costumes and hats, there appears the U.S. Patent date, February 20th 1894 and the words "Copyrighted by Raphael Tuck & Sons Co., Ltd."

Another known Raphael Tuck set, Belle of Saratoga, was used as an advertising doll for Malto-Peptin Bread.

Household Ranges, "My Lady Betty."
(Raphael Tuck & Sons) $55-65

Household Ranges, "Winsome Winnie."
(Raphael Tuck & Sons) $55-65

Fairy Soap, N. K. Fairbank Company, New York

"Have You a Little Fairy in Your House?"

The Fairbank Company made other brands of soap besides Fairy, such as Santa Claus and Gold Dust.

The 1899 wrap-a-round doll, in color lithography, was from a set of six die-cut dolls issued by the company. The only advertisement on the front of the doll is the bar of "Fairy Soap" she is holding. The reverse side of the doll has directions for obtaining the company's premiums. The dolls were mailed free of charge for five Fairy wrappers. The set was printed by American Lithographic Co., New York.

Fairy Soap, N. K. Fairbank Co., doll, 1899. $15

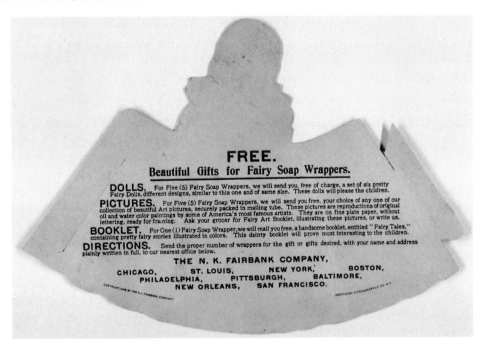

Fairy Soap, reversed.

The Blue Ribbon Soap Premium Book issued by Procter and Gamble listed a paper doll, two dresses and hats for ten Blue Ribbon wrappers. These dolls are like Selchow & Righter's Mamie, Katie and Flossie dolls. Procter and Gamble's premium issued doll has one less costume and hat than Selchow & Righter's doll.

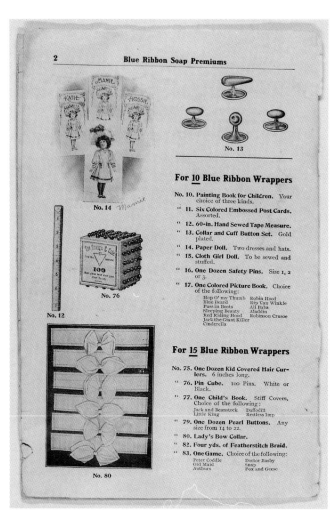

Blue Ribbon Soap, Procter & Gamble. (Premium Book page 2, paper doll—Selchow & Righter's dolls) $10 Premium book

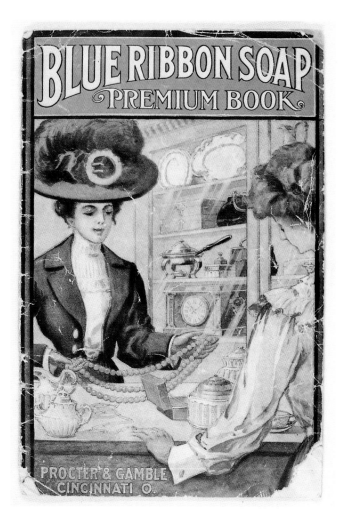

Blue Ribbon Soap, Premium Book Cover.

Boraxine, J. D. Larkin Company, Buffalo, New York

*"A Laundry Necessity
Saves Cost and Labor"*

The manufacturers of Boraxine offered easel-back cut-out dolls with extra costumes and hats in color lithography. The Boraxine advertisement appears both on the easel stands for the dolls and on the hats. The directions for cutting were printed on the doll's sheet and were lost in the cuttings.

Boraxine, J.D. Larkin Co., girl and two dresses. $15 as shown

Boraxine, girls' dresses and hats. $2-4 each

Boraxine, girls' dresses and hats $2-4 each

Pearline, James Pyle, New York

"Our Mamma's Use Pearline"

The company advertised "Pearline" as the original washing compound. The die-cut Pearline triplets are stand-up dolls in color lithography but the one-piece set will stand alone if folded like a screen. The company's slogan appears on the front of the center doll and the advertisements are on the reverse side.

In 1937, the Colgate-Palmolive-Peet Company produced an 8-1/2" x 9-1/2" cutout book, *All Aboard for Shut-Eye-Town,* in color fast-print. It featured costumes and hats (named for identification) plus other accessories, for the famous "Five Quintuplets," Annette, Cecile, Emilie, Marie and Yvonne. The paper dolls are on the back cover of the book, and the dolls are the punch-out type. Of course, Palmolive soap was exclusively used for the daily bathing of these famous babies.

Pearline Triplets. $25-30

Boraxine, boys' costumes. $8 each

Pearline Triplets, reversed.

Dionne Quintuplets, clothes.

All Aboard for Shut-Eye-Town, 1937, (Dionne Quintuplets) Colgate-Palmolive-Peet Co. $65-75 (paper doll book)

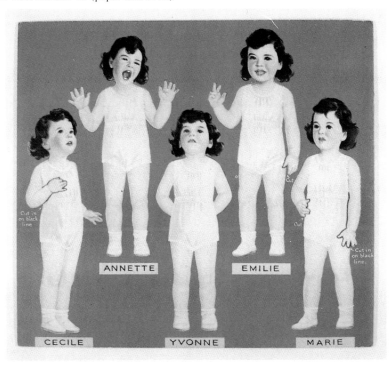

Dionne Quintu-
plets, dolls.

Buttermilk Toilet Soap, Cosmo Buttermilk Soap Co., Chicago

"The Best and Purest Soap in the World for the Complextion
Softens and Whitens the Skin"

Buttermilk Toilet Soap's set of 16 die-cut head-and-shoulder paper dolls are in color lithography. The company's advertisements appear on the back of the dolls, and on the reverse side of each doll's costume. The set was mailed for three two-cent postage stamps.

Buttermilk Toilet Soap. $12 each

Buttermilk Toilet Soap, doll reversed.

"Barney," Behr-Manning, Troy, New York

"Ask Daddy To Use The Sandpaper with Barney in the Triangle."

Around 1930, the Behr-Manning Company offered four different sheets of a cutout bear named Barney, with costumes, in color fast-print. The advertisement appears only on the front, and is lost when the doll is cut.

"Barney," c.1930, Behr-Manning Company. $25

144

Miscellaneous

Pianos, Organs and Music Boxes, J. W. Jenkins' Sons Music Company

"Come to Us for all Your Musical Wants
Oldest Music House in K. C."

The J. W. Jenkins' Sons Music Company, manufacturers of Harwood Guitars and Mandolins, issued die-cut head-and-shoulder dolls in color lithography. The only advertisements are on the backs of the dolls' costumes.

The doll with the disgruntled father and his "colic" baby is similar to the Anti-Suffrage post cards prior to the 19th Amendment giving the American woman the "Right to Vote."

The music company issued two other head-and-shoulder dolls in color lithography, one of a young girl with a yellow cat and another of a girl playing with her stick and hoop.

J.W. Jenkins' Sons Music Co., girls. $10 each

J.W. Jenkins' Sons Music Co., father and baby. $12-15

The Huntington Piano, The Huntington Piano Company, Shelton, Conn.

*"Noted for its
Superior, Tone Qualities..."*

The piano company issued a patriotic die-cut stand-up doll with the American flag draped over her shoulder.

The Huntington Piano Company's advertisement appears on the back, and a local music store owner rubber-stamped his business address on the inside of the doll.

The Huntington Piano Co., girl with the American flag. $10-12

Crown Piano, Geo. P. Bent, Mfr., Chicago

"Oh! how I wish I had one."

The company offered a set of die-cut dolls in color lithography. The five wrap-a-round dolls of different designs each have a different clever saying printed on the front of their skirts such as: "Crown Piano. Oh! how I wish I had one"; "Crown Piano! Oh! Yes, that's the one which has many tones. Mama says no other is like or equal to it"; "Crown Piano! Papa is going to buy me one"; "Doggie & I, Listening to the Crown Piano"; and "The little Queen with her many toned Crown."

An advertisement and direction for assemblage are on the reverse side of each doll. The printer for the set was Gugler Litho., Co., Milwaukee.

Crown Piano, Geo. P. Bent, Mfr. $12

Crown Piano. $12

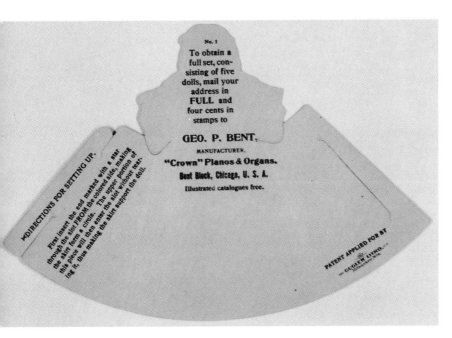

Crown Piano, reversed.

Life Insurance, The Western and Southern Life Insurance Co., Cincinnati,

"Insure Now! Tomorrow May Be Too Late!"

The company offered two cutout dolls on cards 5-1/4" x 3", a boy and a girl, in color lithography. Advertising and directions for cutting were on the front of the cards, while on the back life insurance information was listed.

The Western and Southern Life Insurance Co., boy. $25

The Western and Southern Life Insurance Co., girl. $25

A set based on nursery rhymes pictured "Little Jack Horner" and "Mistress Mary" as cutout dolls in color lithography. The compliment of the company was on the front, and on the back of the card life insurance information was listed. Any life insurance information on the cards was mostly lost in the cuttings. The number of dolls in the set were not listed.

By 1900, the postal service had reduced the second class mail rates, and newspapers began to enjoy an increase in advertising. At this time, many newspapers began to print paper dolls and paper toys as a means to increase their circulation.

The "art supplements" from 1895–1911 period were printed in various newspapers' Sunday editions. *The Boston Sunday Globe*, being the largest distributor, issued a theater setting that could be cut out and assembled, and stage acts were published weekly.

One example was "Little Red Ridinghood," in the December 15, 1895 issue of *The Boston Sunday Globe*.

The Boston Sunday Globe offered, in color lithography, easel cutout dolls with costumes. These dolls have become known as the "Forbes Dolls," and the sets were published in the newspaper's Sunday edition. The two examples pictured are the July 21, 1895 and July 28, 1895 easel dolls.

The Boston Sunday Globe, "Little Red Ridinghood," 1895. $25-35

The Western and Southern Life Insurance Co., "Nursery Rhymes," Little Jack Horner and Mistress Mary. $10 each

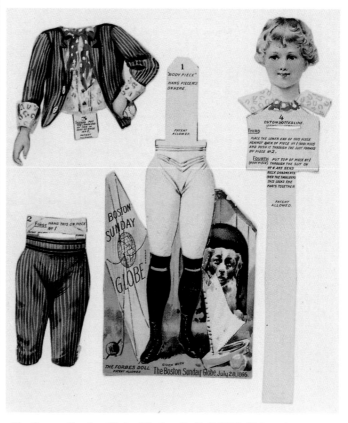

The Boston Sunday Globe, "Forbes Dolls," 1895. $12 as shown

The Boston Sunday Globe, "Forbes Dolls," 1895. $12 as shown

The Boston Sunday Globe also offered cutout dolls with costumes of a historical theme. Examples are Daniel Boone and Kit Carson; Andrew Jackson and Oliver Hazard Perry. These were copyrighted by Woods and Bagshawe, J. V. Sloan & Co., N. Y.

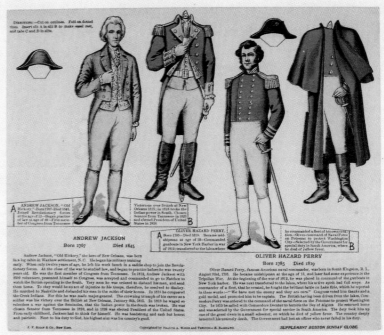

The Boston Sunday Globe, Andrew Jackson/Oliver Hazard Perry. $35

In 1910 *The Springfield Sunday Union* issued a cutout cat, in color lithography, with one costume. The cat is similar to the drawings of Louis Wain, the noted English "cat" artist. Some other animals known to be issued are the bear and the rabbit.

The Boston Sunday Globe, Daniel Boone/Kit Carson. $35

The Springfield Sunday Union, a cat, 1910. $10-12

"Order The Boston Sunday Herald *At Once"*

The Boston Sunday Herald, Fashion Lady June 16, 1895, and August 25, 1895 Wedding Gown. $20-25; $8-10

In 1895 the newspaper printed in their Sunday art supplement a cutout set of fashion dolls in color lithography. The set included two dolls, a fashion figure dressed in pink issued on March 24, and a fashion figure dressed in black issued on June 16. The costumes were published over a period of weeks, and patterns were available for their customers. The March 24th doll is not shown.

Fashion Lady: September 8, 1895 Walking Toilette; and a costume reversed. $8-10

Fashion Lady: August 11, 1895 Afternoon Toilette costume, and
June 9, 1895 Yachting Toilette. $15-18; $8-10

Fashion Lady: Bicycle costume; September 15, 1895 Driving or Dust
Coat; and Bathing Suit. $8-10 each as shown

Fashion Lady: October 27th Opera Cloak, and September 1, 1895
Bridesmaid's Toilette. $15-18; $8-10

Fashion Lady: August 18, 1895 Demi Toilette; and Ladies'
costume. $15-18; $8-10

Fashion Lady: February 9,
1896 Concert Toilette, and
June 2, 1895 Ladies'
Toilette. $15-18; $8-10

Fashion Lady: June 23, 1895 Garden Party Toilette; and Seaside
Toilette. $15-18; $8-10

Fashion Lady: September 22, 1895 Ladies' Toilette; and a Traveling
Suit. $8-10 each

Fashion Lady: October 13, 1895 Ladies' Redingote costume; and Ladies' Toilette. $8-10 each

Fashion Lady: February 2, 1896 Afternoon Toilette; and Ladies' costume. $15-18; $8-10

Fashion Lady: Home Toilette; and Ladies' Toilette. $8-10 each

In 1905 the *Herald* printed in their Sunday supplement a cutout set of "Boy Soldiers of All Nations." The set of 12 figures represented Egyptian, American, English, French, German, Austrian, Russian, Spanish, Chinese, Japanese, Indian and Turkish soldiers.

In 1911 the *Boston Post* printed in their Sunday supplement a cutout set named "Folk Dances of the Nations."

The dolls, Polly and Phyllis, of "Polly's Paper Playmates," series were shown poised as dancers. The ethnic dance costumes were from countries which included Sweden, Switzerland, Spain and Germany.

After 1920, the paper doll as an advertising form gradually began to disappear, as companies started to use radio programs to promote their products.

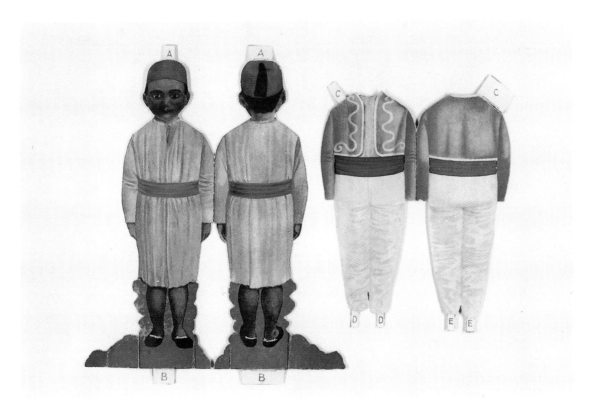

The Boston Herald, "Boy Soldiers of All Nations," 1905, Egyptian. $10 as shown

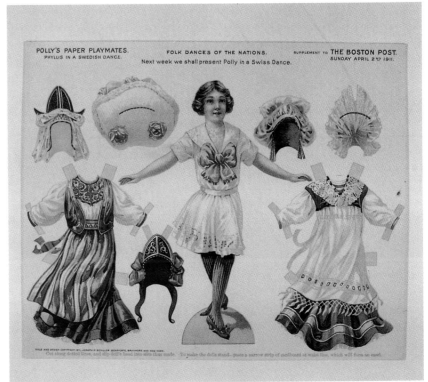

The Boston Post, "Polly's Paper Playmates," 1911, Phyllis in a Swedish Dance. $35

The Boston Post, "Polly's Paper Playmates," 1911, Polly in a Swiss
Dance. $35

The Boston Post, "Polly's Paper Playmates,"
1911, Phyllis in a Spanish Dance. $35

The Boston Post, "Polly's Paper Playmates," 1911,
Polly in a German Dance. $35

Amos and Andy, 1930, The Pepsodent Company

The two die-cut stand-up dolls in color fast-print represent Amos and Andy, the black-faced white actors on the popular "Pepsodent" radio show which aired in 1929. The dolls stand 7-1/2" and 8-1/2" in height. The only advertisement was the small copyright date for the Pepsodent Co., Litho. in U.S.A.

The five-piece die-cut set of characters in color fast-print were given as a premium in 1931 by the Pepsodent Company for their popular radio show. The copyright date and the company's name were printed on the tabs of the stand-up figures.

Amos and Andy, 1930, The
Pepsodent Company. $20-25 each

Charlie McCarthy's Radio Party, 1938, Standard Brands Incorporated

"How To Get The Game:
Send two Chase and Sanborn Dated
Package fronts (or sales slip) and ten
cents to Chase and Sanborn, New York
City. This offer expires November 30th,
1938."

The Edgar Bergen and Charlie McCarthy Show was a popular comedy-variety show which first aired in 1936 on NBC Radio. The promotional game offered consisted of 21 die-cut figures in color fast print, one for Charlie McCarthy, the best known ventriloquist's dummy of all time, and four each of Edgar Bergen, Robert Armbruster, Dorothy Lamour, Nelson Eddy, and Don Ameche. There was also a spinner which determined the play.

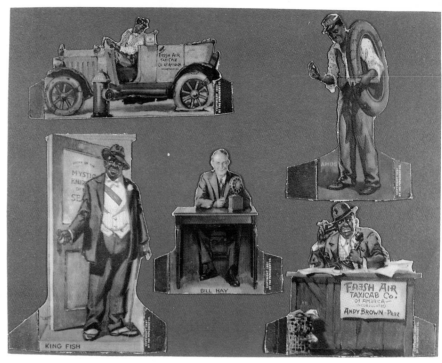

Amos and Andy, 1931, The Pepsodent Company. *Courtesy of Loretta Metzger Rieger.* Set: rare

★ CHARLIE McCARTHY'S RADIO PARTY
DIRECTIONS AND RULES FOR PLAYING

1. The game consists of 21 figures . . . one of Charlie McCarthy and four each of Edgar Bergen, Don Ameche, Dorothy Lamour, Nelson Eddy and Robert Armbruster. Also a spinner which determines the play.
2. The game is won by the player who first secures one of each of the figures (no duplicates) including Charlie McCarthy, or when a player gets all of the figures (20) without Charlie McCarthy.
3. To start, all figures are arranged in individual groups face up in the center of the table.
4. Players spin. The one getting the highest number starts the game. If two or more persons get the same high number, they spin until tie is broken. Order of play is clockwise from the first player.
5. The game is played by spinning the pointer

and following the directions given on which arrow stops. If the arrow actly on the line separating two b player spins again.
6. If a player is unable to complete the play cified, player must pass.
7. Figures taken by a player are placed, face up in front of him.
8. Each play is completed when player releases figure selected.
9. Pointer must make at least one complete revolution.
10. In making an exchange the player must exchange his figure for a different figure.
11. The figure of Charlie McCarthy is moved only when so specified by pointer.

The Charlie McCarthy Radio Game is fascinating and requires a certain amount of skill in playing. While the object is to secure a full set of figures, a player should constantly maneuver his plays so that he will prevent his opponents securing a complete set.

Copyright 1938 by Standard Brands Incorporated

The Charlie McCarthy's Radio Party, 1938, Standard Brands Incorporated, envelope and spinner. Set: $95

Charlie McCarthy and Edgar Bergen.

Robert Armbruster,
Dorothy Lamour, Nelson
Eddy and Don Ameche

Characters in groups of four.

Summary

In the United States a paper toy awareness among collectors during the last half of the 20th century has grown to new heights. The beginning of the 21st century may well see the use of computerized graphic arts setting the advertising trend as did color lithography at the turn of the 20th century.

References

Burdick, J. R. *The American Card Catalog*, New York: Nostalgia Press, Inc., 1967.

Hechtlinger, Adelaide. *The Great Patent Medicine Era*, New York: Galahad Books.

Krebs, Marta K. *Advertising Paper Dolls: A Guide for Collectors*. 1975. (self published)

Krebs, Marta K. "Advertising Paper Dolls." *Doll Reader*, June/July 1979.

Library of Congress. *Preservation Leaflet #2: Environmental Protection of Books and Related Material*. GPO 889-055, February 1975.

Margolin, Victor, Ira Brichta, and Vivian Brichta. *The Promise And The Product*. New York: Macmillan Publishing Co., Inc., 1979.

Marquette, Arthur F. *Brands, Trademarks and Good Will: The Story of the Quaker Oats Co*. New York: McGraw-Hill Book Co., 1967.

Musser, Cynthia Erfurt. *Precious Paper Dolls*. Cumberland, Maryland: Hobby House Press, Inc., 1985.

Ryan, Edward. *Paper Soldiers: The Illustrated History of Printed Paper Armies of the 18th, 19th & 20th centuries*. London: New Cavendish Books Limited, 1995.

Wallach, Anne Tolstoi. *Paper Dolls*. New York: Van Nostrand Reinhold Co., 1982.

Whitton, Blair. *Paper Toys of the World*. Cumberland, Maryland: Hobby House Press, Inc., 1986.

Whitton, Blair and Margaret. *Collector's Guide to Raphael Tuck & Sons*. Cumberland, Maryland: Hobby House Press, 1991.

Heritage Vignette. December 1976, Muscatine Area Heritage Association.

Index